The Dilemma of Democracy
The Political Economics of Over-Government

Arthur Seldon

With a Comment by
Sir Samuel Brittan

Published by The Institute of Economic Affairs
1998

First published in July 1998 by
The Institute of Economic Affairs
2 Lord North Street
Westminster
London SW1P 3LB

© THE INSTITUTE OF ECONOMIC AFFAIRS 1998

Hobart Paper 136
All rights reserved
ISSN 0073-2818
ISBN 0-255 36417-2

Many IEA publications are translated into languages other than English or are reprinted. Permission to translate or to reprint should be sought from the General Director at the address above.

Printed in Great Britain by
Hartington Fine Arts Limited, Lancing, West Sussex
Set in Baskerville Roman 11 on 12 point

Contents

Foreword *Professor Colin Robinson*		7
The Author		10
Acknowledgements		10
Introduction		11
Escapable Government Meets Irresistible Markets		13
Part I	**Democracy at the Crossroads**	**29**
	1. The Government of Democracy	31
	2. The Penalty of Over-Expansion	35
	3. The Disabling Constitution of Democracy	41
Part II	**The Debilitating Disease of Over-Government**	**47**
	4. Over-Government – Too Soon	49
	5. Over-Government – Too Far	54
	6. Over-Government – Too Long	57
	7. Over-Government by Barnacle	61
	8. Over-Government by Stealth	62
	9. Over-Government by Alibi	63
	10. Over-Government by Stampede	64

Part III	The Escapes from Over-Government	67
	11. Escape by Science	69
	12. Escape by Affluence	70
	13. Escape to Personal Services	72
	14. Escape to the Parallel Economy	72
	15. Escape by Barter	86
	16. Escape by Electronic Money	88
	17. Escape by the Internet	91
	18. Escape to the World	97
Part IV	From Political Democracy to Individual Liberty	99
	19. Democracy at Bay	101
	20. The New Mercantilism	102
	21. Too Late to Withdraw	103
	22. The Solution	104
	Table A: Risk and Political Over-Insurance	55
	Table B: Taxation and 'Black' Markets, 1996	77
	Table C: Black Economies in Main Countries	79

Table D: The 'Shadow' Labour Market in Europe	80
Table E: The 'Shadow' Economies, 1960s - 1995	82
Table F: Growth in the Shadow Economy in Austria: The Four Causes of Growth, 1965–1995	83
Comment *Sir Samuel Brittan*	107
References	113
Notes on Trends and Statistics on the Parallel Economy	116
Summary	*Back Cover*

FOREWORD

Over the last forty years the work of public choice theorists has exposed the extent to which government activities grow under their own momentum. Distinguished economists from Anthony Downs onwards, most notably James Buchanan and Gordon Tullock, have shown that people in the 'public' sector are not beings set apart. They have much the same motivations as those in the private sector: to assume that they are especially wise, far-sighted and act only for the benefit of others, suppressing their own interests, does not lead to good predictions of their behaviour. The consequences for the growth of government have been analysed by other economists, such as Sir Alan Peacock and the late Jack Wiseman, who have examined the evidently inexorable upward trend in government expenditures.

The results of such researches have changed the climate of opinion and hence the prevailing view of government activity. For example, both the major political parties in Britain now recognise that government can, if unchecked, become unduly intrusive into people's lives. Governments are beginning to try, if so far not very successfully, to avoid an increase in their share of national income and to hold back a rising tide of regulation.

But, if government activity tends to grow beyond what citizens would freely choose, is it not likely that those citizens will use market mechanisms to escape from the attentions of politicians and civil servants? Governments have powers of coercion but those powers are not absolute. The ingenuity of ordinary people, expressed through markets, normally allows them to shift away from less-desired goods and services to those they prefer. Can not the same be expected if government becomes bloated compared with what citizens would want? Activities can, for example, be moved from the official economy to the 'parallel economy' or from one country to another. With the growth of modern communications, and especially the internet, the power of exit from over-government should be increasing.

It is such intriguing possibilities which are examined by Arthur Seldon – for many years the Institute's Editorial Director – in Hobart Paper 136. As Sir Samuel Brittan writes in his Comment on Seldon's paper, it is a 'characteristically thoughtful piece of work' with the 'innovative feature' of explaining the ways in which people can escape from government.

Arthur Seldon sets his view of the future firmly within an historical context, especially in Parts I-III of the Paper. False arguments about the need for government to supply 'public goods' have provided the intellectual excuse for governments to take control of activities – such as education, health services, some housing provision and some insurance – which the private sector would have provided much better (and indeed in many cases was already providing before the state takeover). For a hundred years or more – the 'lost century' – the state has been encroaching in these areas and crowding out private initiatives.

In 1998, for the first time, Seldon sees early evidence that the British government may be reconsidering its attitude towards 'public' services, as it seeks advice from the private sector in education. But, on the fiftieth anniversary of the founding of the National Health Service, he questions the government promise to retain it for another 50 years. In any case it is, in Seldon's view, very late for any change in attitude to be effective because people are already escaping by many routes from what they perceive to be over-government.

These routes are explained in typically original fashion in Part III of the Paper. Here Seldon shows how people can escape to personal services, to the parallel economy, by electronic money, by the internet or to other countries (without moving because of the expansion of free trade and the impact of better communications). Governments may be powerful but they are not as powerful as market forces. As he puts it in Part IV:

> 'The escapable power of political government meets the irresistible economic force of the market.' (pp. 103-104).

Arthur Seldon will have none of the political arguments to make marginal changes in the size of government nor to make it do more efficiently what it does already – for example, by contracting out or by partnerships with the private sector. He puts forward a far more radical agenda in which the state retreats, cutting its share of national income from around 40 per cent to nearer 20 per cent. If the state does not voluntarily decide to reduce its activities, it will anyway be rolled back by the will of the people. It would be better if government would

> '...arrange its retreat with dignity before the escapes multiply to deprive it of the authority to influence the rate of its withdrawal'. (page 104)

Seldon would therefore like to see a 'constructive reaction...to open markets everywhere'. Government attempts to maintain supremacy over the market have provoked the 'dilemma of democracy'. It can be resolved only if democratic governments rule '...with modest authority that reflects the general will' (page 105): otherwise, it will not be possible to ensure popular observance of that authority.

All IEA publications express the views of their authors, not of the Institute (which has no corporate view), its Trustees, Advisers or Directors. The Institute publishes this Paper by one of its founders as an outstanding and provocative contribution to discussion about the size and role of the state in modern society.

July 1998 COLIN ROBINSON
Editorial Director, Institute of Economic Affairs
Professor of Economics, University of Surrey

THE AUTHOR

Arthur Seldon is a founder President of the Institute. He was its Editorial Adviser and then Editorial Director from 1957 to 1988.

He has had a life-long association with the liberal scholars at the London School of Economics since 1934: as an undergraduate, 1934 to 1937, post-graduate until 1940, a Tutor at the University of London Commerce Degree bureau run by LSE staff, 1946-56, and as a Staff Examiner at the LSE, 1956-66. He had a special relationship with his main teachers: Arnold Plant, Lionel Robbins, Ronald Coase and F. A. Hayek, and continues association with younger teachers – Basil Yamey, Sir Alan Peacock and other scholars.

He has written widely on the application of classical liberalism to industry and welfare in journals and newspapers, in *Hobart Papers*, and in books.

He has been a persistent critic of the state in economic life. In recent years he has been offered honorary doctorates from two private universities, in Britain and overseas.

He is the first, and to date only, Hon. Fellow of the Mont Pèlerin Society and is Founder Editor of *Economic Affairs*, the IEA's journal.

ACKNOWLEDGEMENTS

I have to thank mainly my teachers at the LSE in its heyday in the 1930s, who rose above the faith in the state of its founders Sydney and Beatrice Webb.

In the writing of *The Dilemma of Democracy* I am indebted to all my teachers and friends, and especially three who prompted the book or offered suggestions.

John Davey, formerly Editorial Director of Blackwell, suggested, after *Capitalism*, a study of democracy, of which this is a condensed version.

My economic history teacher in the Sixth Form at Raine's Foundation School in the East End of London originally warned me of the dangers of the state by lending me his student notes on the English Guild system and mercantilism.

And Professor David Conway suggested caution in my forays into philosophy, and especially reminded me of Hobbes's *Leviathan* that caused me to respond with Benedict de Spinoza.

July 1998   A.S.

I. Introduction

Escapable Government Meets Irresistible Markets

After the publication of *Capitalism* (1990), Blackwell had suggested a sequel on the anxieties I had there expressed on the fate of political democracy. It had been exceeding the domain of government acceptable to the people as evidenced by their widening disrespect and failing readiness to finance it. And their evidently growing disaffection could be traced to their increasing ability to escape from its tightening regulations, deteriorating services, and high tax-costs.

*The State is Rolling Back (*1994) comprised 54 essays, since my student days at the London School of Economics, that traced the disappointing tendency of political democracy as it has developed in Britain to generate over-government and its failure to create the essence of democracy: rule by the people.

These doubts had crystallised by the 50th anniversary in 1997 of the Mont Pèlerin Society of international liberal scholars, where I ventured to argue that 'the rule of law' in democracy had not created 'rule by the people'.

'The rule of law' is the covenant of the Western philosophy of liberalism which teaches that the essence of human progress lies in the libertarian process of liberation from restriction whatever its source. This is the political system that facilitates the art of individual learning from experience by taking risks in the unknown. For too long individuals in the Western world have been prevented by over-protective political authority from learning the lessons. Political authority had ended in stifling the freedom to learn. That lesson has in principle appeared to have been learned in the West. But not in practice. Political authority continues to suppress the individual learning process by over-government.

This Paper identifies the dilemma or flaw in the future and fate of democracy and its government.

Economic and political trends since 1990 have reinforced the sense of impending failure: that if democratic politicians did not withdraw their government from over-expanded services and rising taxes to pay for them the people would escape to spontaneous exchange and mutual enrichment in markets. If the rule of law did not underwrite the new freedoms to escape over-government, rule by the people, the essence of democracy, would be established by other means.

Conventional notions on replacing over-government by 'limited' or 'minimal' government seemed inadequate or unlikely. More fundamental thinking on the desirable and likely powers of government in the years ahead appeared long overdue.

For at least some decades ahead, government seems unable to withdraw to its acceptable limits. Its powers to order economic life will be increasingly by-passed where they conflict with the new opportunities opened by fundamental change in the conditions of supply and demand.

This approach differs from ingenious theories (explanations) of government that have attempted to reveal its origins, nature and extent. The title to this Introduction indicates the tension between political power and economic impulse expressed in the natural world *impasse* of 'immovable objects meet irresistible forces'.

Capitalism had argued that the government created by democracy in Britain since the last third of the 19th century had been growing far beyond its indispensable functions. It had enveloped the four groups of 'public goods', 'public' utilities, 'social' services and local government functions that had been conventionally, but as the 20th century developed prematurely, accepted as the desirable and indispensable province of government.

The classical catalogue of 'public goods' – defence, law and order, and lesser functions such as local roads – had been thought since Adam Smith to be necessarily supplied by government. The 'public utilities' – transport and power, water and drainage – were judged to be monopolies best left to the care of the state. The wide range of personal and family 'welfare' services, education, medical care, housing and 'national' ('social') insurance against interruptions in income, were gradually enlarged into a 'welfare state' within the democratic political state. And local government had developed services extending from plausible 'public health' precautions through libraries for the aspiring working man to luxury swimming pools, tennis courts and golf courses.

These 'public' services and functions contrived to create the main impetus and justification for over-government. They have erroneously earned the endorsement of political historians. Belatedly, a counter-development in everyday British life has pointed to a different – smaller and diminishing – role for government. But it has been analysed less intensely by British historians and sociologists.

The neglected historical trend taught otherwise. Early private means of supplying welfare and 'public' utilities that had emerged and developed in the 19th century were spreading in the early 20th century. The trend grew more rapidly after the 1939-45 War, and has grown with unprecedented pace in recent decades and years. Rising private incomes in the past 40 years are now offering historically superior alternatives to the outdated but politically entrenched functions of the over-government generated by democracy.

The development least expected by conventional historians who recorded events without envisaging the likely alternative trends emerging outside government has been the multiplying new avenues of escape from over-government. The tax payments increasingly required by democracy were for services found to be inferior in quality and higher in cost than the competing offerings from outside the state.

Two sources of tension in state services demonstrate the dilemma. Teachers have had to be told by a Secretary of State for (state) schooling, more than a century after its establishment, that they must learn to teach the elements of education that are widely and well taught in private schools. The 'managers' of the state's health services have been told by a Secretary of State that they may be charged at law if they fail to provide statutory standards of service in their establishments. Both Ministers sensed the urgency of improvement but continued their long-held faith that it can be provided by the democratic state.

Government is no longer universally seen as the indispensable sole supplier of goods and services requiring around half of national production and earnings.

It now appears increasingly likely that, if current British government does not systematically withdraw from many or most of the state functions created by its political predecessors, two consequences will be unavoidable. Further escapes to new suppliers outside the state will be sought. And payment – by taxes or other charges – for the superfluous activities of the state will be withheld.

This is the dilemma facing British, and Western, democracy. Its historic predicament is insoluble unless it accepts the logic of its weakening role in 21st-century society. But it may have left its withdrawal too late. If it does not freely allow recourse to better alternatives outside the state its functional ability and moral authority to administer the remaining indispensable 'public' services will dwindle. And it will expose society to the very disorder it was created to prevent. The civic and productive order that democracy was designed to provide will provoke the disorder that Thomas Hobbes foresaw in his 17th-century *Leviathan*.

The question is whether democratic government has failed to see the significance of economic advance. It may have delayed too long the looming withdrawal to its historic role. Its fate is to relinquish the dispensable functions that it cannot maintain from diminishing resources. Its alternatives are order or disorder. If it does not withdraw in good order, by respecting the new abilities and aspirations of the people to escape, it will withdraw in disorder.

If it attempts general withdrawal it will incur widespread displeasure and probably social discord from its beneficiaries, increasingly its remaining employees. But if it maintains its functions it will have to contend with falling revenues from consumers who can escape to better services from a widening range of competitors.

The (so far seven) identifiable sources of over-government are reviewed in Part II and the (so far eight) escapes from over-government in Part III. Both seem likely to be strengthened in the coming century.

Recent trends indicate that it is too late for a British government of any political party to continue raising increasing revenue to pay for the growing services it mistakenly thinks future generations will expect it to supply. If any ironic warning signal is required to discipline government's traditional expectations, it is its latest efforts to raise revenue from practices that British democratic law has blessed with legitimacy. The prospect of pursuing and persecuting taxpayers for (illegally) evading taxes that are (legally) avoidable must make it risk both the respect of its citizens and, more powerfully, their tax payment.

If legally avoided taxes are required to pay for dispensable state services the solution is to change the law in the legislative assembly to transform legal avoidance into illegal evasion. But the main result is likely to be increasing tax evasion, as is now evident from Europe (Part III).

But that is the risk that government requiring more tax revenue must take. If government cannot persuade citizens not merely to obey the written law but also to respect its unwritten *intentions* by treating (some) legal practices as 'anti-social', or by interpreting the intended new 'spirit' of its laws, it is inviting widespread lawlessness. The claim of democracy to live by 'the rule of law' will then lose its legitimacy and could dissolve into ridicule.

In the 1990s economic, technological and political trends have combined and accelerated to weaken the case for the unremitting government regulation of private and family life. The conditions of both the supply of and the demand for many or most of the four groups of government services have been changing more fundamentally than ever since the early 19th century. And the changes have decisively strengthened the ability of citizens as both voters and taxpayers to question the persistence of over-government.

The likely changes are clearly visible. By the early years of the 21st century the people will be able to reject much or most of the functions of government formerly accepted unquestioningly. There will be increasing debate on all four categories. 'Public goods' in defence, law and order, art, culture and heritage will have to justify themselves as necessarily state functions. The 'public utilities' from transport and power to refuse collection and prison administration, misleadingly labelled as necessarily 'public services', will be seen as better organised outside government. The large group of personal welfare services will be seen as better supplied by non-bureaucratic agencies. And most local services will be – are being – better supplied by competing suppliers.

Historians may once have overlooked or understated the early beginnings of many 'public' services in the 30-40 years of economic liberalism in the mid-19th century. Some are rewriting history.

For the first time in British history since the century of state education from 1870 the new British Government has rejected the characteristic fallacy: that exclusive state control was necessarily the ideal objective. In January 1998 it recognised that it could learn from private education by inviting its advice.

If in education the lesson and the same revolution in political thought will before long have to be admitted in all the main welfare services since they all embrace the same fallacies.

The gradually spreading reactions of people in all social groupings have generated resistance, as consumers or taxpayers, both to the intrusion of the state into private lives and its over-regulation of working lives. In the archetypal public goods there is general acceptance of private suppliers of functions traditionally regarded as the province of central or local government. In public 'utilities' the private companies in rail and road, gas, electricity and water, are accepted, not without criticism but with expectation that inadequacies are likely to be removed sooner in competitive markets.

In the 'social' services all four main categories of 'welfare' – education, medical care, housing, and insurance – are losing parents, patients, property-owners, and potential pensioners to private suppliers. There is expansion in private schools, private medical insurance, home ownership despite the period of negative equities, and not least private saving, despite the early over-selling. And local government cannot compete with flexible firms in supplying most urban and rural services.

That the long-outdated faith in 'public' service survives is seen in the latest government proposal for local authority home property valuations to prevent 'gazumping' in house purchase. Politicians in all parties still do not understand the market. Free markets cannot work if their essential mechanism, the ability to offer varying terms until contracts are signed, is suppressed. The next logical step for this outdated purpose would be to put *all* privately-owned homes into local government control as with the five million council houses and tower blocks that few children of their tenants will want as 'homes' in the coming 10 years.

The change from the long-standing state supplier to new private competing suppliers is for most people a new experience, especially the older people who unquestioningly accepted the state services as irreplaceable.

Wider choices have soon freed lower-income consumers and shoppers from sole dependence on government sources. And as producers and earners they can now increasingly redirect their everyday working and earning, buying and selling, saving and investing from the monopoly of the state to the wide range of private competitors. Their interests had been slowly moving from dependence on government from which there was no escape to a range of suppliers that could be rejected if their services deteriorated. There is still no escape from a wide range of government suppliers, from the General Post Office (Royal Mail) for most letter postage to local council housing with millions of 'captive' tenants.

A more unexpected post-war trend has reinforced the lessening dependence on government goods and services. The increasing reluctance of the people to provide in taxes as much as government demands is still not understood by politicians as the growing power of the people no longer dependent on them for most of their services.

The resulting stringency in government revenue has not yet been seen as reflecting the emerging public mood of resentment and rejection. The historic motivations range widely: from the 18th-19th century rejection of desirable taxes by smuggling and other blatant law-breaking, to late-20th-century doubt about the much larger government levies, and now in the coming 21st century increasing suspicion that government services cannot be as good 'value for money' as the competing private services.

The latest scholarly researches into the likely reasons for tax rejection (Part III) suggest fundamental public reaction against the weight and complexity of taxes. And the extensive regulation of economic life has come to be seen as a main cause of the illegal 'evasion' that may now have to be accepted as a wide reaction to the excesses of over-government.

The change in the relationship between government and the people is fundamental to the prospects for democracy. Its representative parliamentary government is no longer seen as the natural, historic, benevolent, sole provider of essential services. It has become a competitor with numerous independent suppliers who have to be more sensitive to individual requirements, expectations, and aspirations.

The state is also increasingly resented as rapacious in its demands for a large share of the people's earnings. And it is no longer accepted or feared as the only source of essential services since the dawning realisation and evidence that government cannot simply command payment by law.

The 'rule of law' has been weakened by excess, by extending it activities where the people believe they are better judges than government and its· agents, however well-intended they may be. The rule of law can no longer express the opinion of government on how society should behave. If the people can withhold payment of taxes government must be more sensitive to the sensibilities of the people.

The resistance to the 1980s 'poll tax' was provoked by the failure to explain that it was a collective tax-charge for local services. Price-charges for personal individual amenities, especially such as tennis courts, swimming pools, or golf courses rarely used by the lower-income ageing residents, would have been more acceptable. The 1997 Government has removed charges for art galleries and other 'cultural' amenities on the ground that cultural education must remain 'free', which means paid by taxpayers who may not visit them, will search for compensating legal avoidance or even illegal evasion. Government has yet to learn that unnecessarily collective 'charging' for personal services that can be paid for by individuals who use them are resented by people who do not. The citizen will always be a step or two ahead of the slower-moving tax bureaucracy.

The new public attitude to taxes marks the deterioration in democracy brought by over-ambitious political leaders. Academics who have long taught that government, composed of selfless, public-spirited saints and seers, must replace the market, must have by-passed the newest branch of economics, 'public choice', that studies politicians as individuals who are no less self-interested than the people in whose name they govern. The persistent error, one of many underlying the continued faith in government, has been to suppose that individuals appointed as public servants have been transformed into public benefactors.

The politicians, ill-advised by academics, have ignored the historic conception of democracy as 'rule by the people'. They have over-reached their role as servants of the people, over-estimated their benevolence, and persistently ignored the seismic changes in the economy that undermine its failing claim to the loyalty of the people.

The long-term changes in the fundamentals of the supply of 'public' services and the demand for them have been obscured by the pre-occupation of government with the short-term importunities of the organised interests whose universal plea of 'under-funding' begs all the questions. Government reactions required to meet the higher standards in goods and services offered by private suppliers too often end in wasteful emergency expenditures, as in patching state schools, National Health hospitals, council homes that will before long be repudiated by the younger generations, and local government services they will condemn as extravagant.

The clearly implied warnings of changing public mood and expectations have been misunderstood or underestimated in political and public, and more surprisingly, academic debate. The interminably rising public revenues demanded by the state have been weakening the mutual trust and respect between government and people on which democracy rests. Yet to maintain its straitened sources of government revenue, democracy is now reduced to the dangerous extremity and historic risk of pursuing taxpayers accused of failing to pay taxes that the courts have judged they are not legally liable or obliged to pay (Part III).

The traditionally law-abiding British citizen is now escaping from the costs of government over-regulation of economic life by recourse to the most ancient as well as the most recent forms of payment that minimise or escape detection. The most primitive, barter, was the earliest trading method, followed by 'cash' in valuable metals or 'worthless' paper, and most lately electronic money and a return to pure barter in the exchange of goods and services without the use of money of any kind.

Combinations of payment can be used in the wide extremes of transactions: from face-to-face exchange to trading on trust with unknown strangers who become allies and friends, not least on the postal or voice mechanisms of the Internet. These are the new world-wide exchanges and trading with mutual benefits between strangers in the universal markets created by the power, identified by Adam Smith, of self-enrichment to enrich one another.

By the 1970s there had been disturbing public disapproval of government encroachment on family efforts to raise living standards. For 30 post-war years the welfare state had employed paternalistic and maternalistic provision, supervision, regulation and admonition in the elemental individual and family requirements of everyday life. Resentment and resistance were stirring. At the Institute of Economic Affairs a new word was coined in 1979 for a study to examine whether, in times when government judged it essential to remove 40 to 50 per cent of the public's earnings, it seemed that the taxpayers' legal minimising of taxes and their illegal rejection of taxes might be inter-related. *Tax Avoision* was the title chosen for a collection of essays by academics and tax specialists to reconsider the economic, legal and moral inter-relationships between 'avoidance' and 'evasion'.

The legal distinction seemed indisputable. The law had proclaimed that practices to reject taxes were either legal or illegal. That established judgement has now been questioned by governments short of revenue and unable to borrow. But the economic and moral differences were less clear.

The formerly unambiguous legal distinction seemed to be obscured by differences between tax-gatherers and taxpayers on the interpretation of the law. The distinction was dangerously blurred in the November 1996, June 1997, and March 1998 Budgets. The anxiety of government to raise revenue by treating legal practices as illegal has stampeded it into weakening the rule of law. The basic economic effects on the production of goods and services might be much the same in the 'official' legal and the 'unofficial' illegal economies. The ironic effects on final real incomes, on the extent of poverty and the degree of inequality in incomes, might be even more economically advantageous in the 'unofficial' than in the 'official' economy (Part IV). Not least, the moral question required judgement on whether the tax-gatherers were levying more taxes than required for the amount, quality and cost of their 'public' goods and services.

The moral question remains. Government may be thought eminently righteous in raising the revenue required for its functions delivered 'in the public interest'. It may also be judged unrighteous in levying more taxes than the taxpayers think its goods and services are worth. In the market this practice is called 'over-charging'. And sympathy lies with the 'over-charged' payer rather than with the 'over-charging' supplier. The difference is that unacceptable government 'public' goods cannot always or easily be escaped by transferring the tax-payment to a competing supplier.

Earlier at the IEA, in 1963, it was thought time to reveal the error in opinion polling over nearly 20 years since the war which persisted in claiming to show that large percentages of national samples – approaching 80 per cent – were ready to pay higher taxes for higher expenditure on state services, especially welfare. Such surveys have continued to appear into the early 1990s.

The simplistic error was obvious to the economist. The samples were not being told the essential information of price – how much in taxes was required for how much more (or better) education, medical care or other services. The crucial information in the economic analysis of supply and demand was simply missing. Without it no taxpayer can answer such questions.

This micro-information, crucial for individuals, cannot be supplied by government, which deals in huge macro-totals. But it is routinely supplied every day in competitive private trading. When prices were introduced into the Institute surveys in 1963, and periodically over 24 years to 1987, the normal rational result emerged: individual taxpayers would spend more for government services if their tax-prices were lower, and less if tax-prices were higher. The higher the tax-price the lower the demand, the lower the tax-price the higher the demand. And, when the tax-price was reduced to nil for 'free' services (or when it was concealed by having to be paid indirectly as taxes), the demand was infinite.

These were the state services that their suppliers accurately but confusingly complained were perpetually 'under-funded'.

When prices were openly stated in the unique Institute surveys it was possible to calculate the degree to which the readiness to pay higher taxes varied with the tax-prices of state services (the price-elasticity of demand) and to attempt a broad measure of the extent to which it varied between higher- and lower-paid income groups (the income-elasticity).

The neglect of price in the familiar opinion polls was, and remains, a surprising failure of judgement in the academic community and a weakness of British public debate in judging the public acceptability or rejection of high and rising taxes. The continuing absence of attention to the extent of the apparently increasing reluctance to pay taxes, which has acquired a long list of labels from 'black' through 'informal' to 'underground' economy and several more, must now be given a morally neutral label to exclude unfounded moral prejudgement. The 'parallel' economy is a description that does not judge how far the propriety or impropriety, morality or immorality, lies with government or people. It is a neutral measure of the various methods of payment and exchange of goods and services, including barter, to arrive at the resulting amount of production, distribution and exchange that takes place alongside the activities and transactions paid in the conventional or customary methods.

The importance of a measure of such 'unofficial' activity is that, because its full extent is unknown, it is generally overlooked or understated in official government estimates of total national production, distribution and exchange. The understatement of economic activity is, moreover, aggregated in international totals, such as those of the OECD. World statistics published by government are therefore mostly seriously misleading: they understate production and incomes, saving and investment, and overstate unemployment and inequality, poverty and deprivation. In short, they make judgement of long-term trends in economic and social life in countries and continents severely defective. For the subject of this study the conclusion follows that misleading opinion polling had encouraged the political parties to expand their over-government to the stage at which its unnecessarily tightening regulation of economic life and high rates of taxation had blindly distorted national and private lives.

Government lacks knowledge of the possibly wide gap between the immediate 'impact' of taxes on its targeted or intended victims and their eventual 'incidence' on strangers whom government cannot trace – buyers or sellers, employees or shareholders, savers or investors, importers or exporters, rich or poor, nationals or 'foreigners'. The so-called 'social justice' of high taxes was among the more questionable consequences of post-war over-government.

From its early years the Institute had reacted against the failure of the universities to scrutinise the economics of large sectors in all four categories of over-government. It promoted early studies of the most neglected welfare services: pensions in 1957 and 1960, housing in 1960, medical care in 1961, education in 1964. 'Public utility' studies began with television in 1962, followed by fuel and transport in 1963, telephones in 1966, North Sea gas in 1967, petrol and other fuels in 1969, and coal in 1974 and into the 1980s when previous governments' failure to adjust coal-mining to changing costs precipitated a minor 'civil war'. Among the so-called public goods, studies of financing local public goods services came in

1963, national public goods in 1964, with studies of defence and crime prevention in 1974.

All four classes of over-extended services had been largely ignored in the 20 years of gradually increasing over-government after the war. And they had largely escaped critical academic scrutiny until the Institute's *Hobart* (and other) *Papers* from the late 1950s questioned government policies and provoked academic, public and political alarm. But government learned slowly. The civil service and industrial obstacles to reform were tenacious. Little wonder that state expenditure financed by taxes expanded almost unnoticed for a further 15 years to the late 1970s.

The most fundamental questions in political economy, many largely evaded in political, public and even academic debate, were raised in these Papers. Yet the expansion in state expenditures was, even into the 1970s, and now in part into the 1990s, defended on the ground that some state services were new and required time to justify themselves. But there were also other neglected effects. Private competing production was inhibited. And government had no information on which to base its claims that its services were superior to all possible alternatives. The disturbing political truth is that post-war British democratic government for a third of a century from 1945 to 1979 felt safe to continue its unquestioned expansion until the belated reaction in the early 1980s and perhaps now again in some forms in the late 1990s.

The continued inflation of government frustrated the most fundamental precepts in the political economy of liberal society. Among the most fundamental recent misconceptions have remained the error, in effect taught by the political class, that government can be the source of righteousness – justice, compassion, equality, and, among the most question-begging, 'fairness', 'decency', and other such undefined offences against the English language. Government has been presented by the politicians of all parties as the all-merciful god of democracy.

The debilitating historic truth that will have to be learned to explain why democracy cannot satisfy its repeated political promises is that its government has grown too large to command the economy by its laws, rules and regulations. The humbling lesson for politicians is that their power to do good or evil is increasingly subject to the private decisions of the people as individuals, families, and private groups and associations of all kinds in everyday buying and selling.

Democracy conceals a fundamental conflict in the efforts of the people to make the most of their abilities and aspirations. Their choices as voters between political principles, policies and sentiments at infrequent elections conflict with their fundamental real preferences as consumers who know costs and pay prices in everyday economic life. Whatever they may have been misled to hope from generous or myopic government they have been slowly rediscovering for themselves, by personal disappointment of state services, performance or promises, the truths of classical liberal philosophy. They are rediscovering that they themselves best know their powers and failings in private exchange of goods and services. And their choices can be made more effectively by the conventional or the newly spreading unconventional means of exchange.

The option is no longer for politicians to tell the people what they will do in government but to confess what they cannot do. The question for the future is increasingly not 'What *should* government do now?' but increasingly 'What *can* government do ?'

As the people escape from over-government the risk for democracy is that it will not long retain the respect of the populace. This is the sobering fundamental state of political economy that should pre-occupy academic, public and press thinking.

The conclusion reached here is that democracy can do no other than withdraw from its over-expansion.

The question is whether it can reduce its insatiable demand for resources and taxes to the amount approved and willingly financed in time to prevent final disillusionment with democracy.

The best hope lies in the early progressive reduction in the power of government over everyday economic life. The required reduction in its appropriation of national income is from over 40 per cent to nearer 20 per cent.

There are enough escapes from over-government for the people to be able to end its long tolerance of over a century. And the escapes multiply from day to day. The political parties can no longer convince the people that they will reject their servitude to long-loyal political supporters, organised allies, public officials, industrial federations, professional associations or trade unions.

The solution in principle is to confess the historic defect of democracy: that, despite its claim to respect the freedoms of the people, it generates too much government. Over-government is the historic defect of the political systems that have dominated economic life: not only socialism in various guises but also the social, liberal, or Christian democracies that claim to practise 'limited' government.

Few democracies, the nearest perhaps Switzerland, have attained the 'minimum' government that confined itself to the functions that the people cannot perform for themselves. Minimum government required it to allow the emergence of maximum market. No democracy can claim to have accepted the limitations of its powers by changing economic conditions.

The ultimate truth and the unavoidable but so far ignored conclusion is that the best hope of preventing the certain excesses of over-government is to prepare for the risks of under-government. And that requires individuals to be allowed in open markets to insure against the risks they should be able to run without obstacles from state over-regulation and over-taxation.

That minimal government with maximal market would entail risks of under-government is the essential difference between over-government and under-government. An indispensable element of reform is to return the judgement of risk from the political process, where it is chronically over-estimated by politicians anxious to enlarge government, to the informed experience of individuals, families, fraternal groups, common interest in everyday private life who bear the consequences of their misjudgements but who learn from experience how to judge and to minimise risks.

The transfer of power from politics to people requires private incomes and expenditure to be raised by no less than a third from 60 to 80 per cent of total national resources. The changed balance of expenditure between people and government from 60:40 to 80:20, halving the 'take' of government, would create the main prospect of rebuilding 'the rule of the people' in 'the rule of *acceptable* law' by guarding against the persistent tendency of democracy to create chronic over-government.

Part I:

Democracy At The Crossroads

1. The Government of Democracy

The failing government of democracy, the results of its over-expansion, and the persistent inadequacies of its constitution are three political weaknesses that remain unresolved.

In the government of democracy no method of representation has yet been discovered to fulfil its historic promise of rule by the people. The Greek 'demos', people, and 'kratia', rule, provided the name but not the reality of 'democracy' as it was envisaged down the centuries.

The 'direct' democracy of assemblies in public squares for debating and voting as in the ancient Athens of the century 400 to 300 BC remains a mirage when government engineers its mandate once in four years to take powers over the details of human life. The 'indirect' representatives of the people to debate and vote in legislative assemblies has produced régimes of political masters rather than servants.

The English civil war between the royal house of the Scottish Stuarts and the Parliament of largely English burghers in the 17th century left the common people with little political power. The reluctant yield by the aristocracy of the vote in the 1832 Reform Act began to give some political voice to some of the people. Yet political power to elect representatives was less effective in spreading self-rule by the people than was economic power of spontaneous exchange. Open markets developed strongly from the late 18th and early 19th centuries precisely because they were largely free of political control. The political liberties of the spreading franchise cautiously enlarged by Parliament in the mid-1800s were more securely ensured by the emerging freedom to use rising incomes for everyday food, clothing, and shelter and later for the early forms of private education, medical care and other welfare services.

For 30 more years from the 1870s until the late 19th century and then into the 20th century economic freedom would have raced ahead of the still slowly widening political franchise. The spontaneous aspirations of the lower-income people enabled them to buy mutual and commercial 'industrial' insurance against sickness, unemployment, old age and the other risks of life.

But the political franchise, although widened to women and younger people in 20th-century democracy, was overwhelmed by the state suppression of the slowly growing economic freedom to buy services wherever they were available in developing markets of competing suppliers. Not the least were the 'welfare' services of schooling, hospitals, the beginnings of home-purchase and assurance of income in the absence of earnings.

The illusion that it was the widening political franchise and representative Members in Parliament that created 'rule by the people' persists to this day. The truth is almost the opposite. Accelerating advance in the underlying economic freedoms and choices of personal and family life have been overwhelmed by the abolition of choice in the services supplied by government, not least those described by the political euphemism 'welfare'. From the later years of the 19th century the people could freely buy food and clothing, beer and tobacco, fuel and transport, but were prevented or discouraged from paying directly for schooling, medical care, or insurance. Henceforward they lost the bargaining power of consumers who paid prices (school fees, insurance premiums) and were reduced to recipients of 'free' services. The irony that many of them paid by taxes was lost in the history books.

Yet the most widely accepted definition of 'democracy' persists in the vision of Abraham Lincoln on the battlefield of Gettysberg in 1863. *First*, it promised democracy by three apparently powerful controls by the people over their faithful servants in the Congress: government would be of the people. *Second*, it would be government by the people. And *third*, there would be government for the people.

None of these visions has been realised. It is too rarely observed in political histories of democracies that, in the original Greek of 'demo-kratia', none of Lincoln's three promises of rule by the common people has been fulfilled.

The political history of the 135 years since 1863 has failed to produce the kind and size of government that creates the required democratic institutions. No democracy, certainly not in Britain, represents even indirect government of the people, the whole people, and nothing but the people. The people have diverse, often incompatible, hopes. No single form of democratic government can create the variegated political framework or environment for diverse life-styles, or accommodate the variety of human preferences. No democratic government allows small groups of minorities to accept or reject its rules and regulations, laws and taxes, and to live as they wish, even where diversity to suit individuals, small groups and minorities is feasible. The notion that its services are for 'the good of the people' where the people could have services that suited diverse circumstances and preferences, is political fiction.

The failure of 'democracy' is evident most fundamentally in the over-used principle of majority. Because it seemed to offer the promise of 'rule by the people' majority decision has been applied both where it is unavoidable and disputably beneficial as well as where it is patently superfluous and clearly undesirable. Because they seemed serviceable in a small range of services, the so-called 'public goods' – public 'utilities', elementary welfare services, and local government services – they were enlarged to cover much of personal and family life where decisions could be taken by individuals, small groups and voluntary associations.

The majority power of democracy is the source of arbitrary rule. Political democracy represents some of the people more than others. Majorities are not only potential tyrannies; they are also often irrelevant, inefficient, domineering, wasteful, intrusive, outdated.

Political democracies based on majorities are encounters of specialisation in political skills. Not the least offensive to the notion of 'rule by the people' is the ability to create pressure on government that yields very much more to the organised than to the unorganised.

The result is a fundamental weakness in the creation of liberty. Democracy has yet to evolve the solution for its central weakness: that the more some people can organise to attract general public attention or sympathy the more they derive advantages or concessions, benefits or subsidies from government at the expense of others who lack the requisite skills. To speak of majoritarian democratic 'rule by the people' is a careless distortion of the English language.

The fatal readiness of democratic government to yield to public pressure has stimulated the formation of politically-motivated organisations guided or managed by professional organisers to create the 'lobby' operating in the wide range of interests from industry, the professions and labour to art, the theatre and sport. They have become a more influential and remunerative profession than university scholarship and its scholars who bestow untold benefits to all the people for untold generations.

The crucial damaging criticism is that the lobbies organise more effectively as producers than as consumers. And producer organisation is easier in longer-lasting staple industries or services – manufacturing, mining, rail transport, teaching – than in shorter-lasting, rapidly changing technology-based trades where individuals make five to 10 changes of employers or industries in a working life.

The even more fundamental human dilemma escapes detection by political analysts. The conflict of interest is not merely between industrial function. It is more essentially a conflict within each individual. Preferences and aspirations are essentially of the personal psyche. Democracy has performed the most unexpected disservice to individual coherence. It has incited many or most people to put their immediate, often temporary, interests as producers before their more fundamental long-run interests as consumers.

In political democracy as it has grown each man, and increasingly woman, is induced to organise against himself and herself. Each is induced to join other producers to extract advantages or concessions from government at the expense of their deeper personal interest as consumer. The conflict is between immediate and eventual interests. The advantages or concessions that raise the price of the product of each man or woman as a producer emerge as costs to him/her as a consumer. And the advantage or concession in a government subsidy for the production of a commodity or service benefits some individuals as producers but eventually injures every individual as a consumer and a taxpayer.

There is a safeguard against such political distortions, but it is a remedy that democratic government has chronically avoided or rejected. The safeguard is to disavow the power of government to grant advantages or concessions. And the institution that most forcibly incapacitates myopic government from such destructive temptation is the open market. This is the only mechanism known to human beings with the unique capacity to restore power to the people by denying it to their supposed political 'representatives' in government. The market enables the people to express their decisions directly and more powerfully than in the legislative chambers of politics. And it is rarely understood that the market emerges spontaneously to remove its defects or 'imperfections' if it is not suppressed by political power.

If the emerging working classes of England had been less seduced by the power to vote for the Liberal and Conservative politicians from the 1860s, if they had demanded freedom to continue building their private schools, hospitals, homes, and social insurance, they would have exercised more influence over their family lives and avoided the eventual capitulation to the disabling social legislation. And the army of 'social workers' would not have had to be the instrument of a government-dominated environment that has debilitated the family and created much of contemporary social disorder.

Government has not been 'of' the people. Neither is democratic government rule 'by' the people. Nor is it government 'for' the people. It has changed from its supposed 19th-century rôle as an avocation for the wealthy into the 20th-century profession that commands high financial or other rewards for its skills of political organisation, management of elections and exercising power in government.

Democratic government cannot react sensitively to the widely varying circumstances of the people. It serves the kind of people who are most tenacious in manipulating the arts of 'politics'. Their causes, from the open interests of industry and agriculture to the disguised 'disinterests' of culture and heritage, the arts and crafts, displace the good of the dispersed people who are relegated to a minor place in the queue for political preferment.

2. The Penalty of Over-Expansion

In recent decades democracy has inflated its powers too soon, too far and too long. It has created over-government even in the two or three recent decades when it was becoming patently even more superfluous.

Its services are now increasingly obtainable from other suppliers with higher quality and lower cost at home and increasingly overseas. And the people, aided not least by science and inspired by the will to be free, are slowly learning to escape from what must more truthfully be re-christened unrepresentative over-government (Part III).

The escape is becoming too widespread beyond the power of democratic government to suppress. The historic 'social contract' between benevolent accountable government servants and their masters, the sovereign people, was ostensibly for the ready payment by taxes for functions and services unobtainable from other sources. This supposed political settlement has been remorselessly dissolving.

What politicians maintain as the necessary costs of government are increasingly sensed as unnecessary costs of 'over-government'. And its taxes, originally seen by William Pitt as income tax, and accepted for a few years as payment for a good bargain, are being subconsciously but finally resented as too high for the quality and relevance of services available at lower cost and higher quality from competing suppliers in the market.

The gradual and imperceptible change in the attitude of the historically law-abiding English is seen in the too-little studied evidence of the European and world-wide growth of diverse forms of tax rejection (Part III).

The historic change in the growing disenchantment of the people with the rôle of government is explained less by the political scientists' analysis of representative institutions, or by the sociologists' pre-occupation with the failure of government to satisfy 'needs', than by the economists' analysis of the contrast between the decreasing value and the rising cost of government, not least in welfare. The political vote of approval by majorities, hitherto the political test of 'democracy', has become less significant than the economic vote of rejection of over-priced government by the people as consumers.

The vital difference between the power of the people as voters and as consumers is too rarely analysed by the proponents of large functions for the democratic process. The voter is the victim of ignorance; the consumer is endowed with unique knowledge. The voter has to accept the intentions of government without evidence of past performance or the power to reject the results of years of power misused. The consumer is equipped with experience of personal wants and the immediate or early power to reject unsuitable suppliers.

The conventional and continuing contrast between benevolent government and rapacious competitors has been revealing in its lack of understanding of the relative power of the voter and consumer. The recent over-selling of saving and pensions schemes was discovered over the years by the very existence of alternative suppliers and the power of the misled to withdraw and move between competitors. The misdescription by successive Governments of the British 'National' Insurance Fund or 'social' insurance as a fund accumulated and scrupulously invested to yield income for payment of sickness, unemployment or retirement 'benefits' was known to Ministers and civil servants for decades but not openly confessed.

The people's choice is not between political saints and commercial sinners; it is between politicians who cannot easily be unmasked or escaped to redeem life savings and businessmen who unmask one another and can be abandoned with manageable loss.

Numerous avenues are opening for more people, especially down the income-scale, to escape from expensive, poor quality, oppressive 'over'-government that democracy persists in supplying in its 'public' services (Part III). The most fundamental escapes are the rising real incomes of the lower-paid and the lower costs created by advancing technology in competitive industry. The least studied are the changing attitudes to the payment for government and the new escapes again evolved by new technology.

The rejection of the historic acceptance, significance and sovereignty of government has widened in recent decades from negligible to substantial. It has been changing in subconscious stages from resigned acceptance of the political machinery to determined rejection.

Historically the legal avoidance of payment for 'public' services has merged into technically illegal evasion and provoked further avoidance that cannot be redefined as illegal. (The relationships between legal and illegal rejection were reviewed above.) The citizen's efforts to minimise payable taxes by changing, reducing or entirely abandoning sources of earnings, not least by early retirement, are beyond the power of democracy to prevent – except by the involuntary labour that British democracy is dangerously approaching.

The leading responsibility for the diminishing respect for democracy and observance of its governing processes is that of the politicians. Even when well-meaning they are misled by the political scientists who have over-estimated the beneficence and intention of democratic government. Political leaders have been interminably invited or incited to expand government, its powers, functions and services, beyond their necessity, beyond their innate low quality, and, not least for the lowest income families, beyond their sheer cost.

By 'cost' the economist supplements the everyday sense of financial payment by the more subtle economic sense of the sacrifices suffered, the alternatives that could have been produced and enjoyed but have been often wantonly lost. But the alternatives in more satisfying services that could been supplied by a more diverse competitive structure of producers and suppliers are rarely discussed by British political scientists or sociologists.

Too little has been studied in the social sciences of the better-quality and lower-cost unknown alternatives – the public goods, the 'public' utilities, the personal welfare services and the local authority amenities – that could have been produced for the people in place of the standardised, impersonal, unresponsive services rationed by government.

And too little has been written, even by specialists in fiscal economics, of the money costs to individuals and families. Government proclaims and publishes statistics of its high spending on 'public' services. Totals with arrays of noughts to reach millions and billions mean nothing to individuals. The fog of figures without individual identity is pursued even into small areas of England. A county town in South-East England proudly informs its local taxpayers that it is spending on local services apparently huge sums expressed in macro-economic millions and billions that, to repeat, mean nothing to individuals.

Yet government is reluctant to reveal the individual micro-economic cost of each service for each service that would enable individual tax-paying citizens to compare the costs of government with the prices of suppressed competing alternatives – from home or abroad (Part IV).

Ignorance of cost and price has been compounded by the widely-used expedient of the concealment of price disguised as 'free' supply. It began in the 19th century as a gesture of compassion for the poor. It degenerated in the 20th into the most disabling obstacle to comparison of costs of government and private services. In the 21st century it may yet become an instrument of secrecy that will further weaken respect for democracy.

The expansion of 'free' government services since the 1939-45 War was all the more untimely since it came in a period of rising real incomes ignored by government. It typified the temptation of democracy to base its policies and institutions on the receding dying past rather than on the evolving beckoning future.

The extension in 1948 to medical care of government service without payment was presented as the only means to ensure that the people would be provided with treatment when sick. It was an enlargement of the illusion that services requiring scarce equipment, labour and land could be 'free' of costs and prices. Yet price is the sole measure, imperfect but unique, of the scarcity of resources and thus of the husbandry required in their use.

The government supply of 'free' services has not miraculously abolished their cost but hidden and destroyed the best available measure of the care required in its use. And it was a further barrier to the comparison of government and competing services.

'Free' government services have acquired the potential of concealing from the sovereign people the alternatives that government can deploy to disguise its political purposes. That government may announce, with pride, that it has transferred £x billions to the National Health Service from other services, without revealing costs and values to individual consumers and taxpayers, conceals the only significant measure of the sacrifice of other services.

Knowledge of price induces the precaution of 'thinking twice'. The destruction of knowledge in 'free' services induces irresponsibility. The 1997 Government sensibly seems to wish to use markets in some industries, but several Ministers seem to misunderstand the twin effects or results of knowing prices. Markets operate with – and reveal – 'income-effects' and 'price-effects'.

The error has encouraged government to emphasise the beneficial 'income effect' and ignore the discipline of the 'price effect' of its measures. The removal of the income-tax rebate on private health insurance reduced the income of the supposed middle-income retired insured subscribers but raised the resulting price-effect that has induced many of them to return to the long waiting lists in the 'free' National Health Service. And by making the lower-income retired patients join the waiting lists for medical care it has intensified the inequality in the long waiting it thought to reduce.

The mis-management of 'income-' and 'price-effects' emphasises the misuse of political power that is now increasingly understood by the people as voters. But democracy will no longer be able to maintain over-government by controls or regulation that are increasingly doubted by the people as necessary or unavoidable.

The dilemma of democracy, hitherto widely neglected by its defenders and critics, has been that it must before long choose between opposites – withdrawing from its over-government of economic life and enforcing it by suppression of the escapes that are opening out. But, more fundamentally, if, as it increasingly seems, it has left the withdrawal too late, its fading resources may require it to replace over-government by under-government.

The 1997 Government has gamely seemed to be attempting both new regulations and relaxations. Withdrawal requires more fundamental re-thinking, but would achieve more than suppression. The argument developed below is that withdrawal is becoming unavoidable if democracy is to retain its popular support or tolerance. So far it has not adapted itself more promptly to social and technological advance. Its future now turns on its readiness to shrink its economic domain, perhaps by as much as a half. If it fails, it faces the even more formidable prospect of waging guerrilla financial war against the people.

The signs of reality vary from the constitutional to the politically pragmatic. The most menacing, for democracy itself, are the efforts to outlaw the legal practice of tax avoidance. The latest is seen in the move against the sale of duty-free goods in the single market of the European Union, universally regarded as its most desirable achievement.

Government initially confronts both a dilemma and a new unknown future. If the escapes from its laws and taxes continue to accelerate, the future of political democracy in which the people as voters elect representatives will fade. Its future will lie in a new democracy based on the power of the people as consumers with power in markets for which government operates the rules required for observance of contracts.

These conclusions are documented and refined below.

3. The Disabling Constitution of Democracy

Democracy is weakened by four central fallacies in its claim or intention to serve the people who elect it. *First*, despite its pretence or intention to take the long view of the effects on the people of its government policies, it is essentially and unavoidably short term in its political thinking. Government is elected or re-elected at the most in Britain for five years, for four years in the USA, for three years in Australia. But economic life continues for decades. No politically conceivable reform – even seven-year parliaments – can enable it to benefit the people in the long term by its wisdom or avoid harming them by its blunders. So they are passed on *après la deluge* to their opposing successors. And both engage in the political tactic of blaming each other.

Party A assails Party B for its '18 lost years' of 1979 to 1997 and '13 wasted years' from 1951 to 1964. In the responsibility of all parties for the political myopia of the post-war years, Party B could have blamed Party A for the 'six backward-looking' years of 1945 to 1951, the 'six drifting years' of 1964 to 1970 and the 'five feeble years' of 1974 to 1979.

Five-year fluctuations in political decisions can disrupt the economic fluctuations over the still roughly 10 years average of the economic cycle between advance and retreat. Moreover, the political decisions of government can affect economic life for the much longer 'secular' periods of up to 30, 40 or 50 years for which firms invest large sums in the production of goods and services to reflect their estimates of the long-term trend in demand for their output.

A *second* weakness compounds the first. Much though the two main political parties differ in their thinking and philosophies, and condemn each other across the floor of the House of Commons, both support the parliamentary system in which the alternating power of majorities predominates in *après nous la deluge* decisions.

This implicit 'conspiracy' against the people is yet another fundamental flaw in the British constitution rarely discussed by the political scientists. For this abuse, as for others, of the political power of democracy the ultimate solution lies in reducing or removing the over-expansion of government.

The *third* weakness of democracy intensifies the conflicting economic and political cycle and the informal conspiracy between the parties. British (and other democratic) governments have the awesome power of patronage to favour individuals and groups: individuals by appointments, influence, monetary awards, titles, and groups in firms, industries, professional associations, trade unions, by subsidies, patents, copyright, preservation of existing jobs, suppression of competition, 'protection' against imports, and more. Yet no politician has the strength to handle such awesome powers and resist the temptation of abuse. The few who have done so, like the scholarly Keith Joseph, have lacked the steel to enact measures they learned during opposition were in the long-term public interest.

The readiness of government to favour vocal organisations encourages the creation of the 'pressure groups' that have become almost an accepted institution of political democracy.

The result is to restrain what would otherwise have been a much faster rise in living standards in the half-century since the last war. And that would have brought a more rapid removal of poverty, a faster reduction in avoidable inequalities, perhaps a halving in the real unemployment in the country as a whole by the readier movement from older to newer industries.

The political motivations of government in favouring production over consumption reverses the natural order of human preference to produce what people want as consumers rather than tamely consume what industry has produced. It thus distorts the structure of industry and the pattern of employment long after its periods of office.

The unavoidable conclusion is that the democracy that is supposed to express the wishes of the people ends by frustrating them because the legacy of government outlives it.

The political submission to established interests and the subjection of consumers to producers is seen most clearly in the persistent failure of government to empower low-income parents to escape from the worst state schools. The teacher trade unions virtually dictate the closed market of 'their' (tax-paid) schools by opposing comparison with fee-paid schools. Yet comparison and judgement by parents could be arranged by allowing parents to transfer the cost of state schooling to schools they prefer. The voucher is increasingly used to create selection between alternatives. Its use for meals, books, and other purchases is teaching the potential power of choice in schooling that could end the disliked social divisions and create the 'one nation' that politicians claim to champion.

The obvious logical way to end poor schools is to empower working-class parents to escape from them. That government has failed to put parents before teachers – consumers before producers – is the characteristic weakness of democracy.

The federal structure of the United States has enabled several states in the North-East to experiment with the voucher's means of escape. With varied experience the more workable methods are being discovered. And among their strongest supporters are black as well as white organisations of lower-income parents.

There can be little doubt that, despite opposition from the American teacher labour unions, the voucher system will spread into more states as the 'public' (state) schools continue to fail. Among its advantages, which could be reproduced in Britain, is that competition from the private schools would raise the standards of the state schools.

A *fourth* weakness of democratic government as practised so far is that it distorts small shifts in public voting sentiment into large differences in Parliamentary seats and majorities. Since the last war winning parties with small, medium, and large majorities have claimed fundamental revolutions in public philosophy justifying massive reconstruction of economic life. Key industries in transport and fuel were made government monopolies. Voluntary initiatives were further depressed, especially in welfare. Local government activities were inflated. Little wonder the unguarded remark of 1945, 'We are the masters now', has echoed ominously in 1964, 1970, 1979, and now in 1998.

The first post-war (1945) Government claimed to have acquired authority for expanding the state. The following Government of its opponents (1951) made the historic error of continuing this pretence. The accumulating over-government misled British democracy into over-estimating its politically moral authority.

The over-government that was begun too soon, was also extended too far, and is being continued too long (Part II). Only now in 1998, after half a century, has democracy begun to acknowledge that the welfare state formed in the post-war years has outlived its day. The 1997 Government has bravely begun a tortuous task of 'modernisation' that will be resisted and may be derailed by its 'barnacles' (below).

Yet its thinking so far is half right and half faulty. It is high time to limit cash payments to low-income recipients. This course, urged in IEA Papers in the 1960s (Introduction), was confidently condemned for 35 years by all political parties and their academic advisers. A clear error now is to put more taxpayers' money into fundamentally flawed services – not least schools, hospitals and housing – that will soon be neglected and rejected.

But the political purse is not guarded as tenaciously as the private pocket.

No post-war government has been given a 'mandate' by the 'ruling' electors to revolutionise the legal-political framework of the British economy and society. The electoral system in 1997 again distorted the relationship between the voters' sentiments and their weight of representatives in Parliament.

The theory of representative democracy – that it creates 'rule by the people' – implies that a change in the number of votes for a political group will produce a broadly comparable change in the weight or influence of their representatives since legislation is decided by their votes. The 1997 Government that obtained 44.4 per cent of the votes has the weight of 60 per cent of representatives. Previous governments exerted similar contrasts between national sentiment and the power of government to change individual lives. Abraham Lincoln would not now endorse 'government of 31 per cent of the people' (44 per cent of the voters).

The distortion in the *quantity* of representatives moreover distorts the influence of the *quality* of the competing arguments. Whatever the competing quality, the Government can by sheer weight of number create the legislation it has designed. The 1997 Government cannot be blamed for continuing the excesses of the political system that elected it. But it is not the democracy of 'rule by the people'. Nor is any other form of numerical representation, whatever the ratios of representatives to people, even if the number of representatives varies proportionately with the number votes. The drawback, much sensed in Holland and elsewhere in Europe, is then that the voter loses personal touch with his representative. Quantitative proportional representatives can reflect public sentiment less than the qualitative personal knowledge of unproportional but known representatives.

There is no known system of political democracy by indirect numerical representation that ensures 'rule by the people'. Not least it compounds the error that majorities are 'democratically' empowered to ride roughshod over minorities. The flawed theory of the precedence of majority over minority is the alleged justification for its use as the best method for measuring opinion on supposedly unavoidable 'public goods' that create benefits all. Elsewhere, in all other goods and services, interest lies in the minorities who require more refined methods of discovering individual and group preferences in families and voluntary organisations.

The 'democratic' political system of deciding government policies by majority voting fails where many or most of its government services are provided for minorities with variegated preferences. The solution lies in the economic mechanism. That is the advantage of the market over the ballot box – whether in general or by-elections, in referenda or plebiscites.

In Northern Ireland hope lay in replacing military by political solutions. The April 1998 political agreement may require the reinforcement of the further market solution that enables minority Catholic families more influence in their choice of privatised schools, housing and other welfare services.

The form of democracy most likely to reflect the wishes of the people decentralises decisions where possible to private individuals or groups. The persistent use of the ballot box, and its enthronement of large groups, has caused embittered social friction and discord wherever it is applied (Part II).

But even the ballot box may fall into desuetude. If political decisions are influence by organised interests to the extent that discussions and decisions are made outside the legislative chamber and in the corridors of stately homes or urban organisations, the outcomes may be too late for the political representatives of the people to influence. Little wonder that the House of Commons has been sparsely attended except on exceptional occasions. And if the representatives who are to ensure 'the rule of the people' are increasingly absentees playing political truant, so may be the electors from the ballot boxes at coming General Elections. They will find that decisions and signals to producers are more effectively made in competitive markets.

Part II:

The Debilitating Disease of Over-Government

Part II

4. Over-Government – Too Soon

Markets are imperfect because they work with and for imperfect people. The instinctive reaction of social scientists is to meet 'market imperfection' by government 'correction'. Their error, even subconsciously, is to suppose that since the purpose of government is to correct error in the market, its well-intentioned performance must initially be supposed to be free from imperfection. Few social scientists are ready to concede that government may be more imperfect than the market. Yet the evidence of history is that the imperfections of government are more deep-rooted and less remediable than the imperfections of the market. The historians persistently overlook three self-defeating tendencies of government that claims to be armed with the cures for market imperfection. *First*, their remedies are begun too soon. *Second*, they are endemically operated too far. *Third*, they are continued too long. The total effect is that governments cannot be adjusted to the advancing superiorities of the market. Crucially they cannot be withdrawn when the market makes them superfluous.

Government remedies are begun before the market imperfections have been removed by growing knowledge of its continuing flow of new, competing alternatives. They are applied too widely to where the market has not yet emerged, but could have been foreseen, to where it is expanding. And they are maintained long after they have become superfluous and could be replaced by the new supplies and demands.

Ample illustrations follow in succeeding pages. The government created by democracy has invariably grown too far because it was originated too soon by a simple error in circular reasoning.

Of the four categories of government activities that have deteriorated into over-government the form that most intimately affects everyday life has been given the most benevolent title, 'welfare', but has most damaged individual and family life. The virtual destruction of the family, not least among the lower-paid groups in the old industrial regions, is the consequence of the usurpation by the state of the authority of parents.

The fallacious pretext for the welfare state from its beginnings in the late 19th century was that desirable services were not being sought by families themselves. This claim is not only historically unfounded. It is rooted in a logical error.

The truth of the origins of welfare in Britain has been surprisingly neglected by English historians. The evidence is demonstrated by 20 authors in two IEA studies: *The Long Debate on Poverty* in 1972, and *Re-privatising Welfare: After the Lost Century* in 1996. The historical evidence shows that by the 1860s most working-class children were at schools paid for by parents with the aid sometimes of the Church or lay charity. By the 1870s some working-class families, especially in the industrial North where wages were higher than in the rural South around London, were beginning to buy their homes with the aid of building societies. By the early 1910s most working-class heads of families were insuring against unemployment, sickness, and ageing. The notion that the working-classes of England neglected their families until the state compelled them by law is historical fiction.

The logical error remains a weakness of a century of British economic and social history. The flaw, still repeated in the latest assessments of the welfare state, is that government had to establish the early forms of welfare state because the people had been unable or unwilling to provide for themselves and their families. Poverty or irresponsibility therefore impelled the state to establish the first 'board' schools in 1870, the first compulsory 'national' insurance in 1911, the first council houses in 1922, the first compulsory health insurance in 1925, the 'National' Health Service in 1948, and other mislabelled 'essential' services in the 20th century.

This neglect of the amply documented history of the common people is the source of the circular reasoning that ironically validated the most conspicuous and persistent growth of over-government. The historical truth is that the precipitate creation of the main (and most minor) forms of state welfare was the very reason why the private forms of welfare, gradually but voluntarily built by the people through 'mutual', 'friendly' and co-operative societies to the 'industrial assurance' of the commercial companies, were in 1946-48 restrained from further expansion. Some were weakened, others expired.

The even more disagreeable political truth is that the state also weakened and finally almost destroyed in Britain an elemental impulse of instinctive Judaeo-Christian compassion – the charitable giving that, as North American experience indicates, would have grown with rising incomes and general affluence.

A sad sequel is the belated rediscovery in recent months of the 'mutual' insurance societies by academics and others who had supported the post-war state policies that almost destroyed them. The recent confession in *The New Statesman* is that 'the non-profit "mutual" and the commercial companies have seemed destined for extinction. But welfare privatisation could yet spectacularly revive them'.

This reversal of historical judgement has come 40 years after Beveridge saw the dangerous toy he had innocently given to the politicians. Only five years after his report on social services in 1942 he was moved to warn of the consequences of political irresponsibility in *Voluntary Action*.

The most regrettable political offence, first, in the premature creation, second, the excessive expansion, and, third, the long overdue winding-up of the welfare state is their weakening of working-class family lives. If, when incomes were too low, the state had provided welfare services 'free' or at low cost, and promptly withdrawn them with social advance and scientific progress, the British 'working classes' would long ago have reached 'middle-class' standards.

Few parents would by now be using state schools when and where they have deteriorated. Few working-class families would now be living in the council houses and none in the mugging enclaves of the high-rise tower blocks. Few or none would be allowing ageing parents to wait a year or more for cataract, hip replacement or knee surgery. And almost all would be reaping the advantages of voluntary insurance with mutual or commercial insurers.

The excuse of low-income poverty might have been plausible until the early 1900s. Professor Michael Beenstock has called it evocatively 'the Lost Century' based on the analysis by Professsor Simon Kuznets: the rising real incomes in the long Industrial Revolution from the late 18th to the late 19th century could have enabled the 'working classes' to pay for the welfare they wanted instead of being tied to the welfare state long after it was outdated. But once tied they are still now being held captive.

The first massive wrong turning, introduced by politicians of the calibre of Lloyd George and Winston Churchill, advised by the academic and later MP William Beveridge, was the introduction in 1911 of compulsory national insurance for working-class heads of families when most were covered, as Dr David Green's researches have revealed. This failure to look forward was government 'too soon'. It dramatises the tendency of politicians to look back rather than forward to the trends or probabilities that would make their measures outdated. The market does not look back. Its critics often blame it for looking forward too far and stimulating 'unnecessary' new purchases.

The opposite error of government 'too long' is seen in the intention of the 1997 Government to maintain the National Health Service for a further 50 years. This political gesture may charitably be interpreted as continuing assurance that low-income older people can expect free medical care for the rest of their lives. But their children will reject the long waiting and general regulatory flavour of state medical care.

The NHS has persistently failed to raise as much financing as the people would willingly pay for advancing medical care without its long waiting. Research from the 1960s to the 1980s into the methods of financing medical care in the mixed systems of voluntary private and compulsory state insurance in other English-speaking countries and Europe has taught that a state medical system would forever remain chronically 'underfunded'.

For decades the mixed state and private financing systems have yielded much more 'funding' than taxes. They have raised some 8 per cent of national income for medical care in Europe and 10 per cent or more in North America. Since the tax-financed British National Health Service had barely raised 6 per cent, it had limited total national financing to 70-75 per cent of Europe and 60 per cent of North America.

By discouraging private insurance the NHS has been the main cause of the 'under-funding' of medical care. British governments have in effect prevented the people from spending as much on improving medical care as they would have wished.

The verdict of the historical research is unavoidable. It is the state itself that created the political 'necessity' for the welfare state. The more welfare it created by taxation (partly re-christened 'social insurance contributions') the more it weakened private financing. The more private welfare it inhibited the more state welfare it had to create.

British government has now so irretrievably 'under-funded' the welfare services that it is in self-made crisis: it must abandon the long-promised state welfare and induce the people to return to private financing. The beginning with pensions will have to be followed in medicine, education and elsewhere. The coming generation of wage-earners will not tolerate for its children the third-rate services that failed its parents.

The state created the pretext for its expansion and has now commendably but reluctantly confessed failure. That it describes measures to save the welfare state as 'reform' or 'modernisation' is more political adroitness of language than historical truth.

The circular reasoning in medical care applies no less to other British state welfare failures. The more 'board' schools the state built after 1870, the more private schools closed down. The more the state expanded its old age pension the less people saved themselves and the less they were helped by charitable organisations. The more local government built council housing the fewer private homes for letting or sale were built by private builders.

The welfare state was a political contrivance: an artificial creation of the state, by the state, for the state and its employees. It is an ironic echo of Lincoln's democracy as government of, by, and for 'the people'.

When its well-concealed but increasing excesses and abuses in central and local government were revealed in recent years, it was after a century of fallacious defence.

The state schools deprived working-class parents of the power to withdraw their children from the worst. The private school parents know that their power to move is the source of their influence on their schools. The power of low-income people to withdraw their children from poor schools, in practice or by intention, was taken from them by the state.

Studies of the inadequacies of state schooling rarely if ever contrast their method of financing with that of the private schools. No further administrative reconstruction by the new Secretary of State for Education, or requiring parents to assist teachers, will improve the standards of the state schools, avoid their wastes of truancy, prevent the physical abuse of teachers, or remove numerous other failings unless he gives parents the power to remove their children.

The superfluous outdated activities of democratic government were continued too long after the 1939-45 War in all four main kinds of state services. The earliest category of 'public goods' were wrongly thought necessarily supplied by government. National defence and 'law and order' seemed the most obvious but others, not least in local government, were expanded for a century until the 1980s.

What are now called 'public utilities' were mostly begun with the rapid growth of industrial towns in the early-mid 1800's. The absence of water and sewage services created anxiety about 'public health' that was then understandably provided by local government or other 'public' authorities. But again they were continued without systematic inquiries into the necessity for long-continued state control.

The third and fourth groups of welfare and local government services have been discussed above.

These are the services established by government too soon.

5. Over-Government – Too Far

After enlarging itself too soon, government expands itself too far.

It has become excessive by over-estimating the scope for its role. Yet it is being followed by a new wave of official paternalism in its precautions and prohibitions against a range of risks supposedly endangering life. The arguable motives range from the laudable anxiety to prevent the spread of infectious or contagious disease to the political purpose of demonstrating government protection of the innocent populace. Since the 1921 classic study of *Risk, Uncertainty and Profit* by the eminent economist Frank Knight of Chicago University, his economist followers have distinguished between costed risk and uncosted uncertainty. Risk is insurable because the probability that it will recur can be calculated from the record of its recurrence. It can be turned into a known cost by insurance, and individuals can judge whether the cost is preferred to the risk. Uncertainty describes the risks

Table A: Risk and Political Over-Insurance
(probability of occurrence)

Possible danger	One in
Struck by lightning	10,000,000
Dying in a 'plane crash	10,000,000
Beef (C.J.D.)	1,000,000
Falling under a bus	1,000,000
Dying in a railway accident	500,000
Choking on food	250,000
Death from accident at home	26,000
Dying in a football match	25,000
Death from road accident	8,000
Death from influenza	5,000

Source: Frank Furedi, 'Obsessed by Safety', *Daily Mail,* 13 December 1997.

that do not occur with sufficient regularity to be insurable.

The uncertainties for which government operates compulsory insurance or outright prohibition by law are generally risks the likelihood of which can be calculated. Dr Frank Furedi of the University of Kent has compared the risks of a range of possible or probable dangers in diet, road travel, freak weather, and others. The chances are one in very large numbers (Table A).

The efforts of government to discover risks and show anxiety to protect the public can be reassuring. But they can be a rich source of apparently beneficial government – and finally over-government. On the day an official Committee announced a possible risk from eating beef on the bone, the British Secretary of State for Agriculture entered the House of

Commons with an official prohibition of its sale. A European Safety Commission has employed 120 researchers into such rare risks as children choking on the small plastic toys enclosed in cereal packets. Britain's Chief Medical Officer of Health has classified unlikely risks:

- less than one in a million - 'negligible'
- less than one in 100,000 - 'minimal'
- less than one in 10,000 - 'very low'.

The risk from beef was officially 'negligible', but democratic government sensitive to public opinion judges that it is wiser to show concern for the voter by issuing warnings too soon rather than too late.

The implications are far-reaching. Three stand out. *First*, low risks can plausibly be decided as ripe for insurance because the cost to individuals in taxes is unknown; not surprisingly, if individuals are asked in opinion polling they are likely to approve of everything they think costs them nothing (below, Section 10). But individuals who bear the cost themselves might have preferred to run the small risk and use the money for a different purpose they prefer. The financial 'free'-dom of the welfare state has been a cause of much ignorance, uninformed choices, reluctance to provide money for improvement and investment, and waste of resources.

Second, the province of the family has been invaded. The authority of parents has again been usurped and weakened in the control of growing children.

Third, experience of risk and judgement of its cost are part of the everyday process of experience and reflection that teaches humans how to live more safely. This personal process is weakened or destroyed if it is surrendered to the political process. Its loss to individuals in private life has been understood too slowly, but private institutions that provided protection against risk by insurance are gradually being rebuilt. A fundamental reconsideration of the role of risk and its management by individual foresight is long overdue.

In his *Song of The English* Kipling wrote of blood as 'the price of Admiralty'. The exploitation of risk is part of 'the high price of politics'.

6. Over-Government – Too Long

There may once have been plausible ground for the establishment by the state of a desirable service that had spread too slowly among the populace.

Even if it had been thought that this historic excuse for a government initiative had applied to the ostensibly most desirable human service of medical care soon after the Second World War, the subsequent years have by now amply revealed that it was also an historic blunder to have continued it for 50 years.

Economic and scientific advance were soon fundamentally and rapidly changing the conditions of the supply and of the demand for medical care of rising quality and prompt availability that would be far beyond the capacity and resources of a centralised, tax-financed organisation.

The 'free' National Health Service established in 1948 can be seen in the light of the subsequent events to have become government activity continued too long. The general rise in real incomes, lagging total state expenditure on medical care, the lengthening queues unknown in any other English-speaking or European country, the continued loss of doctors to the USA and Canada, Australia, New Zealand and elsewhere, improvements in medical science, the growth in private health insurance with early access to medical advice without queueing: all these advances and more would have produced a much higher quality of medical care in Britain.

The characteristic failure and political fiction of 'free' medicine is that for many people with the lowest incomes it has not been available when, where, or how it was wanted. The evidence of history is that it would have been available in all three respects if the government of democracy had allowed it to continue developing as private medicine from its early beginnings.

Yet in 1997, the 50th year of the largely unchanged NHS, it was again reconstructed on the same assumptions of 1947 – that all it required was good-will from doctors, nurses and other staff, and patients would readily accept that all would be well.

The three fundamental fallacies in the faith in the National Health Service were and are still ignored. Not least was the claim, repeated to this day, that it was 'the envy of the world' despite the continuing decision of all comparable countries to reject it.

The further false claim that it offered the highest quality of medical care in the world was obscured by the widespread experience that it was ironically not available at all when it was most wanted. The plausible emphasis on priority for 'acute' cases did not obscure the anxieties, deterioration of symptoms, or the burden heaped on the families of the chronically sick.

Not least the advantage of closer and prompter attention to the culturally advanced higher-income patients who could persuasively argue for earlier treatment than the culturally weaker was not acknowledged by the suppliers – the doctors.

The fundamental economic transformation, largely ignored by the sociologists, was that the National Health Service had replaced a developing buyers' market for medical attention into a sellers' market. That was clear to the economic mind that studied the contrasting bargaining power of buyers and sellers in state medicine and open markets. But neither was it generally acknowledged by the political scientists or politicians who saw only a service that required a periodic infusion of more tax funds. The ailing tax-financing system was made incurable at its core by the lack of guidance from the crucial prices of scarce medical resources that required scrupulous care to guard against over-use.

The plausible but flawed complaint of 'under-funded' obscured the true cause of the inadequacies of the NHS. That truth soon became obvious when in 1968 I was asked by the British Medical Association to join a committee of 10 medical men (with one other 'patient', later a Chancellor of the Exchequer) to recommend fundamental reform in the funding of medical care. Nowhere else in the world, except the USSR and other communist countries, were the people largely limited to state financing of medical care.

But in Britain the internal 'barnacles' – the political, professional and trade union interests – tenaciously resisted reform. Influence on policy lay largely with the doctors as the respected or feared experts whose judgement could hardly be challenged by amateur patients. Economic advance and scientific progress will before long change bargaining power back to the buyers' markets that were developing before the NHS.

The 1997-98 switches of tax funds from some early forms of internal medical markets, which had introduced invaluable pricing, to reduce waiting-lists will not end the periodic breakdowns. The crucial reform is the empowerment of the consumer to escape when dissatisfied. This power will be created by increasing private insurance, emulating his great-grandfather of the 1900s.

British governments have also persistently refused to recognise the embarrassing truth that the quality of state schooling, with exceptions, will not be raised except by empowering parents to escape from schools that ill-educate their children. In the past 50 years governments have fabricated a string of administrative reconstructions that were presented as the final solution but are little more than patching or re-patching of previous government failures.

Here again the lower-income parents often lack the cultural power to argue their case with school authorities. Their grown-up children with higher living standards will in their turn hardly abandon their young to the failing state schools.

Ironically, the superior teaching of the schools that recognise 'parent power' and the ultimate parents' sanction of withdrawing their children, long condemned as 'privilege', is having to be accepted by the long line of supporters of state education. Government is finally inviting the expertise and experience of competing private schools, with the implicit threat of sanctions on recalcitrant state schools held in reserve.

Nor will the families with rising incomes gladly move into the Council houses left to them by the million and more of their parents who bought them on good terms in the 1980s. They will hardly want to live in the Council housing that five million of their parents acquired as tenants even on favourable rents in the past decades. The loss in the capital value of real estate owned by the taxpayers, with large bills for repairs or redevelopment as the costly alternative, will be very large.

It has taken most of the post-war experience to teach the human cost of government that has continued too long. From its earliest years the Institute's studies revealed the coming inability of government to continue its excesses, frictions and tensions. A fundamental limitation on government was its inability to raise the required funds from willing taxpayers. Previous politicians in power sensed earlier doubts, but the new 1997 Government has articulated the fundamental truth that, even if it wished to continue the swelling volume of government activities, the populace were clearly in no mood to pay the mounting bills.

Two political statements show the new readiness of government to accept the change in taxpayer attitudes and powers. The 1997 Prime Minister warned that taxpayers were asking 'fundamental questions about how much we [governments] spend and how we spend it'. And the Minister of Welfare Reform, who has learned from the errors of urging higher spending on people 'in need', has been the most ready of his Ministerial colleagues to warn that the prospect of ever-rising government expenditures has at last ended. Mr Frank Field has had to use graphic language directed at the politicians still hopeful of large and even increasing government: 'We are ceasing to live in a society where taxpayers let us put our hands into their pockets and take out more money.'

The political danger is that his colleagues are advised by academics and others who had urged the high-spending, high-taxing policies over the decades and may too easily relapse into error when the predictable opposition to high-taxing is seen as the signal to low-spending (and low-voting or no-voting).

The task is now to see not only how far normally law-abiding citizens can escape from what they consider unjustified taxation in an economy with over-government. The latest technical devices to detect offenders – road-blocks for interrogation of possible commercial tax-evaders and the 'informer' telephone-lines – could discover some tax-revenue but lose even more by further alienating potential tax-payers.

Government is increasingly caught in the dilemma of democracy. The fundamental conclusion from the evidence examined in this Paper is repeatedly that it is becoming too late for government to withdraw from over-government. Two developments may follow.

It is becoming increasingly urgent to discover new political men, and women, who see the dangers for democracy sufficiently to embrace economic advance and scientific progress in resisting the barnacles. But it may not be sufficient to withdraw over-government to its minimum. To prevent a return to over-government it would be necessary to replace over-government by under-government in which the risks of economic progress from which individuals can learn to avoid or bear are returned from government to the people.

The unresolved dilemma of over-spending and under-taxing has increasingly misled the state for a century. Its fiscal powers no longer suffice, and its moral writ no longer runs, to make 'society' pay for over-government.

7. Over-Government by Barnacle

Trade unions, professional associations, industrial organisations, special interests of all kinds, from artistic to environmental, not only demand increased government expenditure but also oppose reductions that would limit their activities, power, influence, and incomes.

They deploy the most persuasive agents in the most persuasive argument that cannot easily be disproved. Their universal claim is that the activities they favour are 'under-funded': that they could do good with more money.

This repeated formula is an apparent evident truth that throws no light on the distribution by government of the innumerable and unlimited calls on its tax revenues. There are two flaws in the plausible plea from the 'under-funded'. They offer mostly unsupportable claims that their activities are 'vital' for the eventual good of the people – from the spiritual uplift of grand opera sung by wealthy tenors or sopranos, through the preservation of hedgerows by subsidised farmers, to the early rescue from global warming by scientists who could do more good improving the ventilation of working-class homes. And they universally fail to pass the essential test of more 'funding': that it will do more good than in any alternative activity.

The task of government, *which it cannot perform because it deprives itself of the information*, is to decide the good that its allocation of funds will do in all alternative uses. Every human activity can do more good with more resources. Extra expenditure on the arts will produce more or better opera singers. But that is not the important decision for government. It has to demonstrate that the money would not do more good elsewhere. It must therefore show that additional ('marginal') utility in all possible uses has been equalised so that no more 'good' can in total be done by transferring resources from where they do less good to where they can do more.

The result is that all the interests are unconsciously ganging up to force government to continue old activities when they could increasingly be financed by individuals – with the additional advantage that they would know how much satisfaction they received.

The financial acid test of most 'public' services is whether the people for whom they are supposedly intended would pay for them. Let government and subsidised 'public' services be judged not by politicians and lobbyists but by the people for whom they are intended. Let the Royal Opera House, Covent Garden, pay for itself by charging for all seats enough to pay its costs. There would then be less extravagant scenic stages, lower salaries for millionaire international tenors and sopranos, but more charitable prestige subsidies from the banks and insurance companies, and more provincial companies like Kent Opera and Opera Brava for middling-income and middle-brow enthusiasts.

There would also be lower subsidies for farmers on the North Wales hill sides, more young scientists doing more good for the century in which they live than for the next, lower Council subsidies for affluent golfers, and above all lower taxes for alienated taxpayers.

8. Over-Government by Stealth

Of all the expedients employed by the democratic state to require or justify over-expansion of government, the over-exaggeration of risk (Part II) has been used to inflate the use of national 'social' insurance.

The system has now degenerated into an openly confessed deceit as a substitute form of taxation. But even the promise of higher-rate insurance benefits for the widening range of risks to keep pace with inflation has now been accepted by government as inadequate and impracticable.

The state introduced the system unnecessarily in 1911 to cover employed men when most had long been covered by competing private insurers offering a much wider range of benefits to suit individual and family circumstances.

A subtle justification for 'social' insurance is still used, among others by Lord Longford who worked for Beveridge on his 1942 Report, to justify the continued use of social insurance nearly 50 years after it was introduced. Even in the late 1940s it was urged long after the conditions that may plausibly have justified it, as a temporary expedient to provide for continuing poverty, had passed.

'Social' insurance is still a main financial bastion of the welfare state. But its ingenious justification by Winston Churchill – that 'the magic of averages' had come to 'succour the millions' – does not excuse its continuance into the 21st century. Homer nodded. This is the totalitarian remedy of equalising conditions for unequal people. In time it has become apparent that, as Churchill could have said of social insurance when he was Prime Minister in 1951, 'The fiction of averages has come to plague the untypical individual'.

In a growing economy no individuals are widely or permanently 'average'. For people in industries differing in local or international markets, or seasonal employment, or in areas with growing or declining industries the state offered a uniform benefit that was inadequate for some families and unnecessarily costly for others. Social insurance was needlessly uniform. Post-war governments knew, not least, that by the late-1940s and into the 1950s the trend was for millions of employees to be covered by employers' occupational pension schemes. But once the state has introduced new approaches or institutions it cannot easily adapt them to new circumstances. Even if it sees its errors, it is entrapped by the plausible plea that they be allowed time to prove themselves: a plausible excuse for continuing state action when it is out-dated. Lord Longford may not have seen reason in 1998 for the state to remove itself from welfare activities that the people could perform better for themselves. Lord Beveridge quickly saw the dangers 40 years earlier in 1947 when he repented by writing *Voluntary Action*.

9. Over-Government by Alibi

In the early years of the Institute doubts were raised about post-war opinion polling that claimed widespread readiness of the people – often around 80 per cent – to pay higher taxes for more expenditure on state welfare.

By 1963 it was evident that the polls were misleading everyone – not only editors of newspapers but, surprisingly, university academics and politicians on all sides encouraged to win popularity by higher spending.

Yet the fallacy should also have been clear. When pricing was introduced into the IEA field surveys the usual relationship between price and demand was soon revealed: the demand for state welfare rose with lower tax-costs and fell with higher tax-costs.

10. Over-Government by Stampede

Democratic government has been inflated by political over-sensitivity to exaggeration, rumour and confusion on the risks of environmental damage.

The fallacies in the extravaganzas of the environmentalists are mainly five: exaggeration of the evidence, questionable deduction, the confusion between inherent risks (in food or medicines) and amounts or doses, neglect of the costs of prevention, and the allocation of surmised benefit over the unknown generations.

The environmental argument for emergency measures in the 20th century is as fallacious as Thomas Malthus's population scare of the early 19th. It has similar elements of influence on public anxiety: unsubstantiated but plausible warnings of the risk of severe danger to mankind.

Malthus forewarned that the population would grow much faster by geometrical progression, as families more than reproduced themselves, than would the world means of subsistence to feed them which increased only by arithmetical progression in agricultural improvement.

For decades the fear of over-population persisted. But Malthus had under-estimated the rate of 19th-century technological innovation that raised the production of food by much more than the increase in population. Living standards rose faster than in any previous century. The present-day environmentalist overlooks the power of probable but unexpected scientific advance to discover new preventives or treatments for their worst fears without equipping government with more powers that it will not relax when they are found superfluous.

The environmentalists have learned nothing from British history, except the fallacy that government is the infallible instrument of human benevolence. And it repeats the facile failure of other petitioners for the taxpayer's penny or pound – to show the opportunity cost of the alternatives sacrificed.

Malthus's 1798 warning in his *Essay on the Principle of Population* may have restrained the size of families and possibly increased investment in agricultural machinery for food production. The 20th-century environmentalists may likewise induce caution in the preservation of animal and vegetable life. But the most likely expectation is that since their crusade rests on the same over-estimation of risk in all other walks of life, it will add to over-government.

* * * * *

This is a summary review of the (so far) seven main sources of the over-government that would have to be disciplined and abandoned if democracy is to remain the political foundation of Western civilisation.

The opposite tendency is the likelihood that the escapes from over-government analysed by economists will increase in the 21st century. The future of democracy will depend on its ability to reduce its over-government to the size, extent, weight or mass acceptable to the people as shown by their readiness to pay for state services.

The more and wider the escapes (reviewed below, Part III), the smaller acceptable government will have to shrink. The most acceptable size would be that which ran the risks of under-government. Optimum government is better small because it is politically easier to enlarge rather than to reduce too much. And, as the market liberates exchange, it increasingly empowers the people to order withdrawal. Thomas Hobbes's 'state of nature' without 'sovereignty' was a 17th-century nightmare. Democratic market supremacy over rogue government is a 21st-century dawn.

The escapes are emerging from accelerating changes in supply and demand for goods and services that are forming new and more accessible markets outside the control of government for all peoples in all countries.

Part III:

The Escapes from Over-Government

11. Escape by Science

The ability of democracy to create over-government was strongest when the services of government, good, bad or indifferent, were difficult or costly to escape. Defence by the state against external enemies was always inefficient but costly or impracticable to replace by local private defence when the tools of war became complex.

The two kinds of escapes from government services are now growing fast. They are the fundamental universal defences of liberty in economic life – unrestricted access to changing supply and demand. They operate everywhere, seen or unseen. Governments cannot suppress finally them, as the communist régimes of Europe and Asia discovered. But they are most effective and powerful wherever individuals or groups can arrange exchanges with each other in open markets.

The main engine of rapidly advancing sophisticated supply is the discovery of new, simpler, cheaper devices of production and distribution of goods and services tailored to individual circumstances and preferences.

A fundamental deficiency of state services, in the advance of the affluence that is enabling more to escape from over-government, is the cultural difference that paradoxically disadvantages the lower-income families to the benefit of the higher-incomes.

The criticism by Fabian writers of the 19th-century markets for goods and services of all kinds, that they favoured the monied people, was basically valid. The access to the best products was determined or influenced by the possession of purchasing power. The retort of the political scientist Harold Laski to his liberal market colleagues at the 1930s London School of Economics that 'The poor had equal access to the Ritz [Hotel] with the rich' was then true. Yet it stopped short at the ultimate truth that the solution was not to establish a socialised Ritz and supply it universally 'free'.

The truth is that government replaces the old inequality of financial power in markets by unequal cultural power in the realm of the state that is even more difficult to eradicate.

The recent proposal of the 1997 Government to remove the disabilities of the 'Socially Excluded' by easing access to state services would replace them by the deeper-rooted cultural inequality in access to state education, medical care and many more. The differences of family origin, accent, education, occupational connections and the ability to make a case with the controllers of state services are more difficult to remove than financial differences, especially if it is done by lowering taxes and enabling the lower-income people to exercise the same market power of withdrawing their purchasing power if dissatisfied, as higher-income people have long been able to do.

Yet scientific advance is creating easier escape from standardised state services by producing wider ranges of goods and services more easily adapted to individual differences. This sensitivity to individual circumstance and preference would then increasingly spread to the 'public' supply of education, medical care and other services as it has long spread in private competitively-supplied food and clothing, home furnishings and homes, domestic amenities and leisure pursuits that have raised working-class living standards.

12. Escape by Affluence

Rising incomes will enable many families that have passively or unthinkingly accepted the nearest school or the usual family doctor to become better able to pay for services suited to their varying requirements and more demanding in their expectations of school results and medical performance.

Administrative reconstruction of state school teaching and state medicine will not be able to keep pace with the dissatisfaction of parents and patients. The escape from the state will accelerate in the 21st century.

The trend will be especially rapid where children are reared in families that remain cohesive rather than where they succumb to passing fashions in looser lifestyles. The rate of increase in family incomes will produce advances in the home and domestic life-styles of children that will make families more internally supportive.

Moreover, children who have done well in life will hardly allow their parents or more distant elderly relatives to wait endlessly for cataract, hip or knee surgery or endure inferior conditions when sick. They will wish to assist siblings and other relatives with private education. Internal family assistance will extend from unusually generous offerings on birthdays, marriages and seasonal occasions to more formal assistance with allowances to top up low earnings. The family will survive and prosper as the welfare state is replaced by competitive private services.

Internal private redistribution of income was more common in middling-income families than it became after the state nationalised 'giving'. Politicised collective charity through taxation has diminished not only the charitable instinct to succour the needy but also weakened the financial self-help of the family. Charity for the remaining needy and self-help within the family will spread among the lower-income groups in the coming decades.

Of the vast array of 'public' services developed in the 20th century few are now necessarily supplied by government. Some of the so-called 'public' goods, few of the 'public' utilities, very few 'social' (welfare) services, and even fewer local services have to be produced, managed, sold or financed by the political process of democracy.

Around half of all the services, functions, financing and other activities now owned, controlled, regulated or financed by government could be supplied by a widening variety of private institutions. They would be individuals, firms, mutual associations, voluntary organisations, corporations and societies, charities and benevolent groups, and other spontaneous activities that would emerge if the state withdrew from its over-grown domain.

The difficulty has been that individuals and families could not build organisations – smaller, more varied, more personalised – that would create, for themselves or for sale to others, 'bespoke' rather than 'off-the-peg' goods and services. And the difference, even as recently as only 25 years ago, is that most of the services supplied by the state no longer have to be bought from government and paid for by taxes.

It is now possible to escape from most of them, and so halve the reach and writ of government. Taxation could be reduced from more than 40 per cent to less than 20 per cent of personal and private earnings.

The reasons are not far to seek. They are all around us in our daily lives. We are aware of some of the most recent, but strangely oblivious of the most familiar and obvious.

The upward trend in earnings and other incomes will enable more people to buy goods and services of better individual quality than the state can ever provide.

The 'public' goods of law and order can in part be supplied by competing private suppliers. Not the least important, the 'public service' once regarded as essential, is perhaps the least expected. The British are being protected from loss of possessions and personal assault by private police forces. And when the offenders are caught they are increasingly prevented from doing harm by being housed in private prisons and other places of detention.

This movement from 'public' (political) to private has been broadly the trend in our life-times since and before the last war. But the upward trend in quality will now be much faster.

13. Escape to Personal Services

The growth in recent years of the number of people who do not work on the premises of their employers is in large part the result of technologies that maintain communications by computers. It is also, if less clearly, a subconscious intention to escape, or at least to minimise, taxes on earnings, not least by reducing taxable work.

Income earned from services such as consultancy or advisory yields economies of scale in selling to several purchasers who pay by fees rather than salaries. Work that can be done at home rather than at the employer's premises replaces physical transport by wired communications.

The new technical marvels have not yet reached most people. But their children are learning them at school – even, but more slowly, at state schools. And parents will want to learn faster to maintain family communications (below, Section 17).

14. Escape to the Parallel Economy

Over-government is overlooking the opportunity cost of making taxes more difficult to reject by avoidance or evasion. The more successful the measures to maximise tax collection the lower the net earnings in the 'parallel' economy of barter or other methods of escaping taxes as well as in the 'official' economies. But the lower therefore will be the production of goods and services, the more poverty will remain, and the longer inequalities will persist.

The escape from over-taxation has produced a forest of labels to describe the motivations or intentions of the escapers.

In principle, the three aspects of tax rejection – legal, economic and moral – remain in the wide range of labels from 'black', to denote crude defiance of the law, through a string of labels to embrace mixtures of motives – informal, unrecorded, shadow, and others – to the so far little-used but most appropriate term, 'parallel' economy. It emerged in discussion with a Swiss economist on the calculations in the *World Competitiveness Report* and the extent of production outside the 'official' statistics in the reports from the OECD and other international organisations. 'Parallel' seemed the most convenient as a neutral term to describe the 'unofficial' production of national product and income. The total of 'official' and 'unofficial' ('parallel') economies would then measure the full range of productive activities and complete the calculations of total production or incomes. The term 'parallel' also avoided moral judgement of the responsibility for tax rejection, whether government or people, the taxers or the taxed.

For neutral observers analysing the economics of productive life 'parallel' avoids the allotment of moral responsibility between the government tax creators, for over-estimating the readiness of taxpayers to share their earnings with government, and the individual tax rejectors, for declining justifiable taxes. Economic interest lies in the total production of the goods and services that raise standards of living, diminish poverty, reduce inequality and have other beneficial effects, whatever the motives of the producers.

To work with taxpayers who like paying taxes must be the understandable hope of every new politician who enters Parliament to win appreciation and power from the electors.

The accord between the policy-makers, who decide their electors' payment by taxes, and the taxpayers, who cannot assess the services of monopoly government, can be judged only by the readiness to pay taxes without question. Government services, taxpayers should think, are good value; 'we' elected 'them'; so we should pay for what they give us without complaint.

The historic democratic compact, the 'social contract' between government and people, was based on the voluntary exchange of government respect for the people and the people's trust in government. It reflected the acceptance of government decisions and the taxes it levied as necessary for good order. Historians have yet to study the changing relationships of mutual respect between government and people in Britain. The past century of growing over-government, and its implied disrespect for the capacity of the people to learn from liberty, to make decisions, to assess the unavoidable uncertainties in human life, to treat adults as children who have failed to grow with experience, have created disillusion with 'democracy', mistrust of politicians as a self-appointed superior breed, and fomented reluctance to pay their taxes.

Neither government nor taxpayer has to sell to or buy from the other most of the services they exchange. For some taxpayers mutual respect has been increasingly replaced by doubt and resentment. The evidence is the emergence of numerous varied trading devices that facilitate the (legal) avoidance or (illegal) evasion of taxes.

The latest development in government methods to detect tax avoiders or evaders – road-blocks to question suspected drivers and 'informer' telephone lines – may garner modest amounts in taxes from small traders and occasional evening or week-end earners. But they raise anxious questions about the relationship of trust between government and people and the role of politicians as servants or masters of the people.

In the relationship of buyers and sellers of services over-government has bred indifferent politicised suppliers and reluctant consumer-buyers. The transformation from mutual respect to mutual suspicion, the estrangement between government and people is the natural reaction of consumers faced with a monopoly – 'public' or private – that betrays its lack of confidence in itself by denying escape to competitors. The Chancellors of the Exchequer in their budgets of November 1997, June 1997 and March 1998 sounded new notes of aggrieved unpaid creditors rather than as suppliers of services on good terms with their satisfied prompt-paying customers.

The manageable 'black' market of the inter-war and early post-war years has been replaced by widening varieties of tax-rejection that defy the easy descriptions of politicians and government officials. It is no longer sufficient to imply a deep moral gulf between virtuous tax-creators and venal tax-resisters. The gulf was long called 'black' to emphasise the contrast or conflict between government and people. The 'informal' or 'shadow' economies implied a lower degree of conflict or contrast. The 'underground' better conveyed the French spirit of war-time resistance to oppression.

The more recent term that avoids moral judgement between government and people – the 'parallel' economy – requires a more searching analysis of the necessity and defects of taxes.

A straw poll has been attempted by recent governments to gauge the general sentiment on 'public services' based on the series of Charter undertakings to supply high quality with penalties for failure. In 1997 it requested, from the real 'public' of the people, nominations of 'Charter Mark' awards by government to organisations judged to have given good service. The Cabinet Office or its nominees received 29,000 nominations for 10,000 local services. The 1998 Charter Mark scheme circulated examples of services that might qualify for nomination:

schools
the police
ambulance services
fire services
doctors
dentists
hospitals
clinics

local library
leisure centre
refuse collection
housing
benefits agencies
job centres
tax offices
others

Nominations could be for (one or more) awards of a Charter Mark in six categories of satisfaction:
    'excellent' service
    complaints promptly settled
    staff helpful and polite
    'efficient' service
    service beyond expectations
    other reasons.

Nominations could be submitted by post, telephone, on the Internet by E-mail or to the web-site. Evidently more of the public know the Internet than is commonly supposed.

Whatever the substantive value of the Charters, which must be questioned since they list aspects of services long assumed to be the very purpose of 'public' services, or the authenticity of the nominations, it is clearly difficult for government to know how far general taxpayers or specific beneficiaries are content. There are no alternative services with which taxpayers can compare them. Nor is there return of taxes to dissatisfied recipients. The value of this effort to gauge public satisfaction must remain unestablished, especially in terms of its costs, the small response and the obscurity of the nominations.

The satisfaction of taxpayers must ultimately remain to be measured by their willingness to pay taxes for government services. Neither government nor academic students of the fiscal system knows how many pay their taxes gladly, why some pay little or nothing, or their reasons. The parallel economy, which produces no taxes on a wide and accelerating range of productive activity, is surprisingly little studied by political scientists and sociologists, or even by economists who judge the production and distribution of national income without the large part that is unrecorded or under-assessed in official government statistics. It is not surprising that so far little is known about its causes and extent.

Three substantial reports on world economic trends have offered information on varying aspects of the parallel economy. The renowned *World Competitiveness Report*, 1995, an absorbing study directed by Professor Stephane Garelli of the University of Lausanne, was primarily concerned with the elements of economic activity that strengthened or weakened comparative national economic dynamism. A cautious reference to the reluctance to pay taxes may be inferred from his observation that, despite the growth of global competitiveness, national citizens may be 'keen to decide upon environmental, social or medical protection... [or] to subsidise culture or agriculture ... through taxes'. He thought they 'may have preferred to run massive public debt...', the alternative to taxation that had doubled in Europe and the USA in the dozen years to 1995. This massive rise could reveal that it was politically easier to levy taxes on the taxpayers of the next generation, who cannot vote against them, than on their living parents, who know the present pain of reduced incomes after taxes.

Two further world reviews were more explicit on the extent of the less legal forms of tax rejection. The *1996 Index of Economic Freedom* from the Heritage Foundation of Washington

DC defined 'black markets' as explicitly outlawed by government and graded their rejected taxes. They are shown (Table B) correlated with the taxation of broadly similar countries:

TABLE B: Taxation and 'Black' Markets, 1996
(as percentage of GDP)

Country	Taxation (grade)	Black Markets (grade)
New Zealand	3.5	1
France	4.0	1
Australia	4.0	2
USA	4.0	1
Canada	4.0	1
UK	4.5	1
Austria	4.5	1
Sweden	4.5	1
Netherlands	4.5	1
Japan	4.5	1
Germany	5.0	1
Italy	5.0	1
Spain	5.0	3

Tax grading: score 3 - top income tax rate 35 per cent or less
average taxes below 15 per cent

score 4 - top income tax rate 36-65 per cent
average taxes 15-20 per cent

score 5 - top income tax rate over 50 per cent
average income taxes 20-25 per cent

Black market grading:
score 1 – 'very low level'
score 2 – 'low level'
score 3 – 'moderate level'

Source: 1996 Index of Economic Freedom, Heritage Foundation, Washington DC.

The sources for the tax gradings were recent reports from the World Bank, *The Economist* Intelligence Unit and the accountants Price Waterhouse.

The gradings for 'black market' were also assessed as components of illegal activity: the extent of smuggling; how far technical appliances (video-cassette recorders) were sold by 'black'-market traders as evidence of prices raised substantially by tariffs; or workers in illegal activities, as evidence of over-regulation.

These largely outlawed activities exclude the productive economic life of the wider parallel economies which comprise tax rejection as a whole, whatever the inducements or motives. Their incomes may include cash payments – 'tips' and others, rents from tenants, self-employee profits, under-estimated or under-stated consultancy 'fees', barter between individuals or firms, and others.

The total parallel economy is probably much larger than the 'outlawed' activities in many countries, especially perhaps in Sweden, Italy, Spain and others.

Illegal 'black markets' as identified in the Heritage Reports are created by government laws and regulations. If the parallel economies are substantially larger than these estimates of around 5 per cent for 'illegal' tax evasion (for advanced countries unofficial guesses rise to 25 and 30 per cent of GDP - below), governments in many Western democracies have estranged large segments of their normally law-abiding populace. Some light on the causes of their reluctant tax rejection has been shed by further researches (below).

The third world report, for 1997, was prepared for the Fraser Institute of Vancouver and 47 institutes world-wide by Professors James Gwartney of Florida State University and Robert Lawson of Capital University. It intends to examine these further aspects of tax rejection in future Reports.

Higher estimates are offered in the annual *Economist* predictions in its *The World Economy in 1998*, described as 'Black Economies' (Table C).

The *Economist* material emboldened its Editor, Dudley Fishburn, to pronounce: '...every country's unofficial black economy will [in 1998] do better than its government statistics will show.' Its reasons for the 'black' economies are listed as high taxes, onerous labour market regulations, red tape that induces 'scorn of officialdom', social insurance, sales taxes, cash pay to employees ('often illegal immigrants'), and 'paper work' registering a new business. The 'shadow' economy was a 'healthy response to excessive government interference', but in 1998 tax-leviers would 'crack down harder', which would raise the costs of 'legitimate' business. The better solution would be to attack excessive regulation and high taxes, otherwise revenue would dwindle.

Table C: Black Economies in Main Countries
(per cent of GDP)

Country	
Switzerland	6
Japan	9
USA	9
BRITAIN	12
Germany	15
France	15
Sweden	18
Spain	23
Italy	24

Source: The Economist: *The World Economy in 1998.*

The latest evidence has come belatedly from the European Commission in its report, *Communication on Undeclared Work* (extracts published in *The European*). The EU document is far from as informative as it could have been but it provokes searching questions and inferences. Its estimates are shown in Table D.

The EU report is informative on the numerous devices, some ingenious, agreed between employers and employees, to make and accept payment in cash. Its general conclusion, predictable from an international association of governments, is that the solution is '[government] intervention oriented towards punishment'. The EU has yet to accept that stricter government enforcement may produce less rather than more tax revenue.

The European output that escapes the tax net is estimated to be produced by 10 to 18 million officially 'unemployed', from the high-paid to the low-paid, many of whom may also work as well as claim social benefits.

Table D: The 'Shadow' Labour Market in Europe
(per cent of GDP)
(approximations within wide margins)

Greece	35
Italy	26
Spain	23
Belgium	22
Germany	14
France	14
Netherlands	14
BRITAIN	12
Ireland	10
Denmark	8
Austria	8
Sweden	8
Finland	5

Source: European Commission, *Communication on Undeclared Work*, reported in *The European*, 6-12 April 1998.

The European's headings to its review may seem overdramatic: 'Millions are moonlighting to make ends meet' and 'Going underground is a worker's last resort'. Yet the mounting evidence of widespread alienation from democratic government seems incontrovertible. The European Union's 'official' total of 18 million unemployed in Europe is almost certainly much too high; 11-12 million would be nearer the true estimate.

What remains to be identified are the diverse causes of the disaffection. Here the most refined researches and analyses have come from Friedrich Schneider, Professor of Economics at the Johannes Kepler University in Austria. His work was discussed at conferences of the European Public Choice Society in the 1980s. British economic policies in the 1970s and earlier had been producing evidence of resentment and resistance to intrusive high taxes. Clearly a fundamental reconsideration of the economic, legal and moral aspects of what seemed a growing part of economic life had become long overdue.

As with many other neglected subjects the IEA was first in the field with *Tax Avoision* in 1979 (above, Introduction), a hybrid title for the hybrid development in fiscal affairs, assembled shortly after a further IEA field survey in 1978 based on prices that cast continuing doubt on the conventional price-less opinion polling.

Professor Schneider had written in a 1980s issue of *Economic Affairs* a general review of the extent of the shadow economy. In the September 1997 issue he analysed a more detailed study of 18 countries from the 1960s to 1995, including 11 of the 17 in the OECD. His findings for the 'shadow' economy from various dates in the 1960s, 1980 and 1990, with my imagined projections for 2000 and 2010, are shown in Table E.

Professor Schneider's 'demand for currency' method of measuring the 'shadow' economy is based on the proposition that, because cash transactions are easier to conceal than payments by cheques, credit cards, and other records, the larger the amount of currency in circulation, the larger the probable 'shadow' economy.

The 'currency-demand' approach is the most widely-used method of estimating the 'shadow' or parallel economy but omits some forms of tax rejection. Cash is not required for the growing device of barter (Section 15). Objectionable regulations weaken the sense of obligation or exacerbate defiance in paying taxes. Cash in American dollars is virtually an international currency held by people in other countries. The frequency with which currencies are used (the velocity of circulation) probably varies even more in the full parallel than in the official economies. The size of parallel economies in the years before the first of these estimates is not known. The estimates are calculated on the generous assumption that there was no tax rejection in the preceding years, so the estimates for all countries are probably far too low.

In spite of these unavoidable limitations the estimates indicate the widespread increase in the shadow economies over recent decades. And the omissions (cash, barter, and so on) make the full parallel economies possibly much larger than the other 'unofficial' economies shown in the Tables.

To improve the estimates derived from the limited 'currency-demand' method, Professor Schneider persisted with further refinements, incorporating the researches of other economists, of the statistics available since 1965 for his country, Austria. Moreover, they indicated the likely main causes of the increases over 30 years, which is a rare finding in the researches into the causes of payment and non-payment of taxes.

Table E: The 'Shadow' Economies, 1960s - 1995
(Measured by the demand-for-currency method)

Country	First date	1980	1990	2000	2010
Austria	0.4 (1960)	3.1	5.3	7	10
Belgium	7.8 (1965)	15.4	19.6	21	25
Canada	6.5 (1975)	10.7	13.5	17	21
Denmark	4.3 (1960)	8.6	11.2	15	20
Germany	2.1 (1960)	10.8	11.8	15	20
France	3.9 (1970)	6.9	9.4	12	25
Italy	8.4 (1965)	16.7	23.4	28	36
Netherlands	4.8 (1970)	9.1	13.9	19	25
Norway	9.5 (1960)	10.6	15.3	20	30
Spain	18.0 (1978)	21.0	21.0	32	40
Sweden	1.7 (1960)	-	12.2	15	20
Switzerland	1.2 (1960)	6.5	9.9	12	17
UK	2.0 (1970)	8.4	10.2	14	19
USA	3.4 (1960)	5.0	6.9	8	12

Source: Friedrich Schneider, 'The Shadow Economies of Western Europe', *Economic Affairs*, Vol. 17, No. 3, September 1997.

These causes are undoubtedly adaptable to other countries in Europe. It remains for us in Britain to attempt similar calculations and establish more accurate estimates than existing government statistics or guesses.

Four main causes were detected in the more precise statistics for Austria: *first*, the weight of direct taxes, *second*, the

**Table F: Growth in the Shadow Economy in Austria:
The Four Causes of Growth, 1965-1995**

Year	Total Shadow Economy % of GDP	Direct Taxes	Indirect Taxes	Complexity of Taxes	Intensity of Regulation
		\multicolumn{4}{c}{*per cent of causation*}			
1965	1.16	51.2	12.1	25.9	9.8
1975	1.73	50.9	15.9	23.4	9.8
1985	4.16	44.0	25.2	15.2	15.6
1995	7.20	28.7	26.6	18.7	26.0

Source: Schneider, *op. cit.*

weight of indirect taxes; *third*, the complexity of all taxes; and *fourth*, the intensity of detailed government regulation – of industry and private lives. The estimated total shadow economy in each decade from 1965 to 1995 and the four causes are shown in Table F.

The movement in the figures over the 30 years 1965 to 1995 could be repeated for Britain to indicate the reforms urgently required to reduce the British shadow economy. They are: lower direct taxes, lower indirect taxes, simpler taxes, and more comprehensible regulation of industry.

The figures yield intriguing results. The effect of the direct taxes, which were the most potent of the four causes throughout the 30 years, has fallen from the mid-1960s, when it accounted for 51.2 per cent of the shadow economy, to 28.7 per cent in 1995, and was then almost overtaken by the intensity of excessive regulation, 26.0 per cent.

At a time when the British Government is concerned about the loss of tax revenue there is here unique crucial guidance in fiscal and general financial policies.

The apparent influence of indirect taxes in Austria doubled from 1965 to 1995 to account for a quarter of the shadow economy. This trend could be traced in Britain to reveal the responsibility, if any, of VAT or other indirect taxes for the growing parallel economy.

The Austrian tax system seems to have been simplified since 1965, when its complexity apparently explained 25.9 per cent of the shadow economy, and fell to 18.7 per cent in 1995. There is undoubtedly room for simplification of taxes in Britain.

Yet the most striking change in Austria has been the trebling in the intensity of regulation of industry and economic life generally, which increased its responsibility for the shadow economy from a tenth in 1965 (9.8 per cent) to more than a quarter (26.0 per cent) in 1995. This is another warning to Britain about a main culprit in its expanding parallel economy. The growth of almost mercantilist detail (Section 20) in its restrictive regulations of industrial and private life is a clear case for close examination.

Professor Schneider's work shows the degree of refinement in searching for the radical causes of what is becoming instinctive tax rejection. It should be applied in Britain before the Government can assess the full extent and probable causes of the shadow and parallel economies. This task is an essential preliminary to the fundamental reconsideration of British taxes and regulations that the Government seems to be attempting in adjusting the welfare state to the 21st century.

The remaining doubt would then be whether the growing disinclination to pay taxes would resist the obstruction of the required reforms. Government may have to accept that British taxpayers will not tolerate the taxes and regulations of past government to deal with painful adjustments to economic change or to satisfy the chorus of 'under-funding' from vested interests.

Methods of estimating parallel economies will undoubtedly advance over time. The inter-actions between the 'official' and 'unofficial' economies are emphasised by Professor Schneider as an early task of research. Lower taxes in Austria in the late 1980s, which might have been expected to reduce tax rejection ('avoision'), was followed by increased rejection. Either taxes were not reduced sufficiently to satisfy taxpayers or the increasing habit of rejecting taxes has been fortified by the new technical and financial methods of escaping from them.

It may be concluded that it is too late in Austria, and in Britain, to solve the democratic dilemma, the choice between reducing over-government despite the widespread displeasure of beneficiaries, or maintaining it despite the disaffection of taxpayers and the loss of their revenue. The solutions may go further than yet contemplated by Western democracy: the unprecedented political acceptance that government is not able to ensure compliance with its 'rule of law'.

The obstinate truth is that the growing parallel economy may reflect deeper resentment of taxes that is beyond government influence to discipline unless it withdraws from large stretches of government activity. It may be that the 1997 Government, which shows new readiness to embark on unexpected welfare reform, will find that it will also have to withdraw increasingly from most other services in public utilities and familiar local facilities that no longer satisfy newly affluent families who can find better services in the market.

Whether there is still time, or it is too late because its superfluous functions can be escaped, are considered in Part IV. For a Government laudably ready to take advice from scholars researching into the empirical evidence for overdue reforms, employing British economists to emulate Professor Schneider's researches could show whether there is still time.

So far British government has been complacent about the distortions in economic life that will continue if the harmony between government and governed is not soon restored. It will not least entail acceptable relationships between the 'official' and the 'unofficial' economies. The 2000 figure for the British parallel economy will probably be 10 per cent higher than all other estimates. A total parallel economy approaching 25 per cent of national income is likely unless taxes are reduced much more than now seems probable and regulations are relaxed rather than tightened as implied in the new mercantilist mood in health, safety, rural building, environmental and other precautionary policies.

Non-payers of taxes are increasingly productive citizens. Smugglers, pedlars of drugs, young women from families weakened by the welfare state, and other long-familiar categories, may be increasing. But non-payers of taxes outnumber them as typically self-respecting men and women supplementing taxed earnings by evening, week-end or spare-time services in domestic, secretarial, research work, or sitting with the sick, the old or the young, some paid in cash or by swapping skills and spare time.

An obvious improvement in research on the (illegal) evasion of taxes continues to be neglected. For some years surveys questioned recipients of wages, salaries, fees, fares, tips, and other payments whether or how far they were paid in cash. Understatement of earnings was likely. Surveys that asked payer-employers how much they had *paid* in cash would yield more authentic information (Marjorie Seldon, in Seldon, A. (ed.), *Tax Avoision*).

This approach indicated three improvements on the conventional opinion polls. *First,* it was more reliable since it inquired into the cash paid rather than received. *Second,* it inquired into what the sample had done in the recent past, not into the what it might possibly do in the remote future. *Third,* it covered a wider range of work and indicated the range of participants who regard themselves as supplementing family income 'in their own time' and would be offended to be categorised as law-breakers.

Such surveys might cause Chancellors of the Exchequer to be less severe in levying taxes. Before long they might find that lower tax-rates yielded higher tax revenue.

Accountants with little training in the elasticities of demand for labour and income may see only the non-observance of government edicts. Economists and political scientists might then theorise on the size of government that maximised the yield of taxes accepted as justified to finance its more modest expenditures. And moralists might analyse the relative responsibility of tax-leviers and tax-rejectors for the strains in government financing and political democracy.

15. Escape by Barter

The latest form of probably unintentional or unconscious rejection of taxes is the exchange of goods and services, or of goods for services, that arise in the normal course of social relationships between friends, neighbours or members of societies or other associations.

Barter has shown three stages. It was the earliest form of primitive exchange before the use of money. It is a development of informal exchange of services or experience based on custom or tradition among the members of a profession, often medicine, a specialism, possibly engineering, or academic abilities, usually in the social sciences, to share developments in thinking or information from research.

The exchange of services, advice or information is 'free' of charge. The intention is mutual aid or stimulus to new thinking. But the unintended effect could be a significant escape of taxes.

The exchange of gestures can easily develop into more systematic organised exchange of goods and/or services that avoid the use of money and are technically barter.

Sooner or later the unintended consequence is a conscious acceptance that both parties are in effect not paying taxes on the monetary value of the income in kind of the goods or services they exchange. The clear result is that the higher taxes are raised the more valuable the informal exchange or formal barter and the stronger the inducement, even if subconscious, to bypass them.

The third development in the unintended non-payment of taxes is the widening use of tokens generally accepted to avoid the inconvenience of arranging exchanges between strangers. People who do not know each other but have goods or services they would willingly exchange can accept tokens. In time the tokens become 'money', which is simply a convenient, generally acceptable 'means of exchange'.

But it is a device which is evidently being found to have wide applications. In the last four or five years it seems to have spread across Britain and attracted the attention of the national newspapers, and mostly lately broadcasting.

But little is known about how far it has spread. It may well be reaching more parts of the country with new forms of 'money'. Nor is it clear how it can be stopped if government believes it may one day significantly reduce its tax revenues.

Not least, it is difficult to conclude that even as a natural expression of sentiment between individuals, it should be outlawed by government which upholds the liberty of the subject. For individuals to choose to express gratitude towards one another, even if it impinges on the ability of government to supply so-called 'public services', is a seemingly harmless sentiment that government restricts only with risk of disturbing communal harmony. It may set a limit to the amount of individual resources that government can safely claim without forfeiting the public respect on which democratic government ultimately depends.

When at a seminar of economists and political scientists in early 1996 in Yxtaholm, Sweden, the highest-taxed country in Europe, the judgement was ventured that barter could one day become a substantial leakage of government revenue if taxes incited resentment, it was met with incredulity. A highly respected economist from Switzerland indulgently thought it might be an 'early shoot' of an economic trend in foreseeable developments in the European Union.

A similar sceptical reaction came from a former British Government Minister at a 1997 conference of liberal economists in Spain. When he emphasised the widely different extents of unemployment between Britain and mainland Europe the 'official' figure of 18 million was described as unrealistic; in view of the double income of the so-called 'unemployed' – from unreported employment and national insurance 'unemployment' benefit – I suggested that the true total might be no more than 11 million.

The exaggeration of unemployment also applies to most of the countries that solemnly submit their official national statistics to the OECD for unchecked republication.

We may never know how wide-ranging the rejection of taxes will evoke a more rapid and extensive resort to barter approaching that of the more common legally-proper tax avoidance leading to illegally-improper tax evasion. If taxes in Britain remain unchanged, or are not appreciably reduced, it nust be accepted as a clear possibility that tax rejection will expand to the volume it has reached in the higher-taxed countries of Spain and Italy.

The decisive uncertainty for the future of democracy is its ability – or failure – to rein in over-government to the 'optimum' amount that the people are freely willing to pay for in taxes. And here they may prefer not only less to more government; they may also take a chance on too little government that they can expand rather than the too much government they cannot discipline once it takes root.

16. Escape by Electronic Money

If the relationship of trust between government and people is replaced by growing conflict between over-government and the people's impatient rejection of high taxes, the search for new ways to elude detection by the tax-inspectors and tax-collectors may be expected to grow.

Although payments by cash are seen as a way to elude tax-paying, a 'cashless society', in which payments are made by electronic 'clearing' of debits and credits between banks and other specialists in financial balances, would seem to make rejection of taxes even easier. Such a method of simplifying payments has been discussed by economists in the USA for some 20 years since the Automated Clearing House (ACH) was developed experimentally by the American Federal Reserve as a way to simplify payments.

Its possibilities are still being judged. In late 1996 Alan Greenspan, the Chairman of the American central bank, the Federal Reserve Board, foresaw an increasing rôle for electronic money at a US Treasury conference on the rôle of government in the supply of means of payment. His address on 'Electronic Money and Banking' concluded that, although electronic money was likely to play a smaller role than that of the private money of currency and cheques, history indicated that government should allow freedom to experiment in the new private currency markets of the 21st century.

It is the comparative freedom to experiment in the unknown, even in unknown means of payment for goods and services, that has made the USA the richest country in the world, with far less poverty and inequality than the countries of Europe. Here, except for recent short periods under Erhard in Germany and the then Mrs Thatcher in Britain, we have retreated to the government-enforced security of 'safety first' that makes for indifferent economic performance.

As in other sectors of the economy, industry, trade and welfare, the historic interrelations between government and the market in the inventions of new kinds of money and credit have been misinterpreted. The general inference is that 19th-century markets had been inadequate or undesirable and were rightly replaced by government in the 20th century. This is the precise opposite of the deduction more accurately drawn from the experience of providing private money in America.

The main lesson is that competing private suppliers of private monies had voluntarily evolved rules and procedures that protected the public from the misdeeds of the suppliers of private monies.

The conclusion drawn by Greenspan was that the private market should now not be inhibited by government from refining experiments in providing private monies. The historic truth, difficult for democratic politicians to defend, was that private monies had misled the public far less than US Governments in their debasement of government money by recurring inflations.

The evidence of history until the recent British inflations of the 1960s and 1970s is that the *non sequitur* 'market failure, therefore government correction' is still applied to money as to almost every other act of government. Yet 'government failure' has invariably been more ineradicable than 'market failure'.

Greenspan's conclusion in 1997 echoed the rigorous theoretical argument of Hayek in 1976. Ultimately the only certain way to prevent government debasement of its money means of exchange was to 'privatise' it. He called it 'denationalisation', by which he meant de-monopolisation by transferring it from the sole monopoly control of government to competing supply by banks or other issuers of private monies.

Hayek's 'theory' (explanation) of competing monies was impeccable. It supplied the missing link in preventing the supply of money from causing inflation by outrunning the output of goods and services. The sophisticated rules devised by the monetary economists to prevent the over-supply of government money and so inflation relied on the integrity of politicians who had often succumbed to inflation, not least in post-war Britain. After their misdeeds in office they had retired with titles and well-paid consultancies.

But the private suppliers of money proposed by Hayek would suffer financial loss, bankruptcy, public disgrace and worse because their money would lose value if issued beyond the amounts required to lubricate trade and exchange.

Hayek's solution remains the only way to prevent the debasement of government money until, if ever, it is replaced by electronic money.

Scientific advance is now making electronic money more convenient than existing forms of currency in cash or cheque. In the 21st century growing disaffection with taxes as payment for unsatisfying government services may lead to further refinements in payment by book entries.

Greenspan foresaw that electronic money would allow payments or banking instructions to be sent increasingly over new networks such as the Internet. It now seems likely that government over-taxing and over-regulation (a major inducement to tax rejection, Section 14) will encourage the invention of new forms of money, electronic and others, beyond cash, cheques, even barter. And law-abiding citizens will use them more as they are refined to serve the four classical functions of money: a medium of exchange generally accepted in payment for goods and services, a unit of account to permit comparison of their value, a store of value that does not deteriorate with time, and a standard of deferred payments.

The essential is that government does not prevent the emergence of new forms of payment. Greenspan argued that private monies should not be prevented from evolving methods of 'self-policing' by frequently updated credit ratings and other devices to prevent abuse. The early 19th-century experience had shown how markets behave when government rules are not 'pervasive' and private suppliers can adapt their trading to changing circumstances.

High-value payments in commerce are likely to be increasingly electronic. But, despite the spreading use of credit cards, everyday consumers still generally pay with paper currency in cash or cheques and are alert to the inflation of rising shop or direct mail prices. It is here that the suppliers of 'private' branded monies will come to be seen as more secure than government and its 'official' monies.

Government cannot deny its disreputable record of intermittent inflations, even in Britain in our day, and their far-reaching evil consequences. The warning from Greenspan against the financial susceptibility of government is stark:

> 'I am especially concerned that we do not impede unduly our newest innovation, electronic money, or more generally our increasingly broad electronic payments system.'

17. Escape by the Internet

Intrusive and oppressive government has almost miraculously had to acknowledge a new adversary in the most unexpected technical marvel of the 20th century.

A recent sample inquiry to the Internet 'web' produced around 46,770 'searches' into the 'Informal Economy' in countries as varied as Britain and the USA, Mexico and Mozambique. No doubt more would have been found under the range of labels from 'black', 'shadow', 'underground', and many others, though possibly not many so far under 'parallel'.

Other labels would yield higher numbers. But only a half of word processors are so far connected to the world 'Web'. The scope for expansion challenges the imagination.

Not least, the latest scientific world marvel of the Internet is advancing at such a speed that it is rash to assess its rate of advance in the 21st century. The key will be whether it accelerates faster than the other 'escapes' from over-government.

The Internet has been described by Alan Greenspan as 'unprecedented in providing versatile, low-cost communication capabilities' – American for simple ways of establishing contact between individuals all over the world. The Internet 'web' is the most remarkable technical advance on the two 20th-century inventions that have revolutionised the means by which strangers communicate – and trade – with each other: the telephone for sound and television for sound and sight. That is the not disinterested view of the most adventurous Internet entrepreneur, Mr Bill Gates, which seems likely to be as near the truth as that of his competitors. Even if the expansion of Gates's Microsoft product is for a time retarded by opposition to his 'monopolistic' tactic of conditional sale with an ancillary component, there can be little doubt that the use of the Internet as a whole will continue to grow probably faster than both the telephone and television.

It will be used in everyday personal life for shopping and entertainment as well as in trading. Every business – industrial, professional, legal, and financial, small and large – could be connected. Young people, even children, are taking to it faster than adults.

By late 1997, one in 10 US adults, 22 million, were using the Web at least once a day; the British equivalent was so far perhaps three million.

The Web will cost time to use to the full, but it will also save time by discovering information almost instantaneously about intending purchases. It will thus raise what Hayek called 'the discovery process' of the free market, still often 'imperfect', to unimagined heights of 'perfection'.

No-one will have to pay more than the lowest possible price anywhere in the world. For the theme of this Paper no government will be able to charge more in taxes for its services than the market can supply at lower prices around the globe.

That must be a sobering reflection for politicians who still see the national political process as supreme over all other developments. The essential truth they must reluctantly but increasingly accept in the years ahead is that government does not provide the people with a procedure of discovery comparable with the market. Government does not furnish a mechanism by which it can compare or contrast its prices with those of its competitors.

Yet in the early years of the 21st century government may be required to acknowledge the truth that its prices are often higher, even where its products are inferior in range of choice, quality, or the failure to refund (tax)-payment if the taxpayer customer is dissatisfied.

That realisation may lead to further public awareness of the inefficiency of government and political acceptance of the sobering truth that government products are worth markedly less than their tax prices.

That may lead to a public demand that government add one final 'free' 'public' service that will enable the taxpayer to compare government and competing prices. So far the information that central government and its local agencies supply to taxpayers is a mass of macro-economic totals which convey little or nothing of comparative cost and value. Local government taxpayers who are regaled by expensively-printed brochures telling of the millions or billions of pounds spent on schools or libraries, refuse collection or fire services, are expected to interpret these impressive strings of noughts as evidence of careful expenditure by wise local Councillors on well-run services. The sobering truth is that they tell local taxpayers nothing of the ('micro-economic') comparative prices and costs of excluded competing private schools or libraries, refuse collection or fire services, which can be lower, especially in Europe or North America. An average-sized county town in the South-East of England proudly tells its taxpayers that it has spent their Council taxes on 'vital' or 'essential' services (listed in order of amounts):

Housing benefits -	£18,214,000
'Other services' -	£ 6,927,000
Planning and economic development -	£2,511,000
Recreation and Tourism -	£2,344,000

Refuse collection -   £1,187,000

Cleansing services -   £1,167,000
(streets and public
conveniences)

Environmental health -   £965,000

Local taxpayers would be more enlightened if they could compare the local tax costs/prices of such services with the market costs/prices of competing private services.

The early announcements of the 1997 Government were also mostly 'macro-economic' totals. The millions or billions (of pounds) 'saved' by the Secretary of State for Health on the 'bureaucratic' internal medical markets were transferred to 'patient care'. The millions or billions 'saved' on the Assisted Places Scheme 'got rid of' by the new Secretary of State for Education were spent reducing class sizes. Without knowledge of comparative individual costs the claims made for these supposed wiser ways of using taxpayers' money were precarious.

The Internet is more revolutionary than the average citizen knows. Mr Gates writes his e-mail correspondence on a 20-inch LCD (liquid crystal display) monitor which will be cheap enough in two years to sell to the general public. But in 10 years a 40-inch LCD may be commonplace. Other now unexpected, and perhaps now unimaginable, advances will also then be everyday occurrences. And scientific advance will have removed the Web to safety from the police control or restrictive regulation of political government.

So much for the view of a producer. A graphic but authoritative account of the spreading Internet by a discriminating consumer is no less mind-stretching. The distinguished American journalist, Andrew Sullivan, has eulogised his 'wonderful web life'. The Internet has become not only 'an economic or scientific event [but] a genuine cultural shift' by reaching 'a critical mass of users...accessible to all'.

That stage has been reached in competitive America. It seems slower to reach corporatist Europe. The resistance to technological innovation is natural for established industrial, managerial and employee interests in Europe that may be disturbed by them. Yet economic advance is brought to life by the open market and can no longer be suppressed by government.

The advantages of the Internet for humanity are disturbing to the conservative mind, which invariably ignores the benefits that would be lost - to the poorest as well as the richest. Mr Sullivan dramatises them as a user newly awakening to its potential. The most popular Internet service, America Online, is used by more young and middle-aged people (aged 17 to 49) than listeners or viewers of network news programmes.

It has created 'a new era'. He, and many like him, communicates more by e-mail than by telephone. He 'e-talks' to his family, doctor, editors and stockbroker. ... The world's [news]-papers are 'delivered to my screen, free. I chat with strangers...Who [he may offend his British opposite numbers] needs pubs?' For £60 his computer camera and video software enable him to talk live with anyone with the same technology anywhere in the world. 'Once you've bought the equipment, usage is free. I haven't bought a book in a bookshop for a year. Every possible title arrives at my door within two days...I sent my mother flowers with a click [on his personal computer]...I buy airline tickets, socks, no longer write cheques, pay bills, taxes, ...I can buy stocks for £6.' Who, the British investor may ask, needs a stockbroker for £100?

The wider economic and political benefits foreseen by this graphic observer are even more dramatic, if perhaps more arguable:

> 'The full consequences ...[include] the immense boom in the American economy... When information is as accessible as this...the world shucks off an ancient barrier to communication...growth booms, prices fall...It's capitalism by keyboard.'

'Capitalism by keyboard' is a dramatic slogan that the defenders of Western capitalism, long cowed into silence by the century since Marx and Engels, could now use in harmony with Yelstov.

Many observers may remain sceptical of such awe-inspiring technology. It savours of the 'irresponsible' activity outside the ordered political arrangements with foreseeable consequences created by the rule of law of the political state. But it may prove to be the most liberating technology invented in the 20th century with unforeseeable expansion in the 21st. Its 'anarchic' structure, says Sullivan, 'is the most striking testimony to America's capacity to generate new commerce and culture from the chaos of freedom'.

'The chaos of freedom' comprises the institutions that permit the politically unrestricted entry of new buyers and sellers to meet and enrich each other in free markets.

This vision illuminates the economic conditions that permit the emergence of unpredictable change, advance and progress. It is the debilitating failing of the non-economist who does not understand that all progressive human life emerges from unavoidable uncertainty. It is the crippling effort of government to introduce 'order' that excludes avenues of discovery, advance, progress, with rising living standards for all, from the poor to the rich.

Mr Sullivan's *chaos of freedom*, rarely understood by the critics of the market, dramatises the system of free exchange between individuals that explains the innate power of free markets to produce progress. And it explains the unavoidable fate of 'ordered' society produced by the over-government of socialism and social democracy to degenerate into loss of freedom and lagging living standards.

'Chaos' theory is a development in economic thinking that is revolutionising the natural sciences. It explains how the apparently unforeseeable fluctuations in human reactions, which seem irregular, reveal broadly regular predictable trends. The human reactions emerge by a process of learning from the experience of uncertainty. Human beings who know their immediate circumstances more than outsiders learn to adapt themselves to the uncertainties of life better than political authority can enforce by regulations. It is simplistic to suppose that uncertainty can be foreseen and controlled 'in the public interest' by centralised, short-termist, biased political judgement.

In America the Internet, says Mr Sullivan, has opened up a new frontier 'of complete democracy and limitless anonymity' in which the individual is not subject to crippling law framed by irresponsible, uninformed 'democratic' politicians . He is now empowered to 'reinvent himself not merely twice in a lifetime but [on the Internet] *twice in an hour*' (my italics). People can 'renew' themselves as often as they can 'change their [Internet] screen name'.

Government will crib, cabin and confine the human spirit no longer. In the Internet

> 'there is no government; and, as yet, no taxes. As Britain fast becomes the second country to join this Hayekian [*sic*] paradise, Britons may soon discover they are getting more than a convenient way to check on their stocks. They could - virtually - enter the [same] state of anonymous nirvana'.

It is to be expected that national governments, perhaps in league with other governments, will attempt international regulations to maintain knowledge and influence, controls and restrictions on these developments. The more likely trend is that science and the human spirit will remain two or three decisive steps ahead of the slower-moving machinery of international politics.

18. Escape to the World

In the history of mankind the world has providentially offered escapes from poverty and oppression. In our times the New World of North America remained 'New' to the peoples of 'Old' Europe whom it welcomed or accepted in their desperate search for relief from the poverty of Tsarist Russia or the savagery of National Socialist Germany.

These escapes required the risks and fatigues of moving families of young and old from 'Old Europe' to unknown lands and homes in 'New Europe'. The New World of science that empowers individuals to escape from ignorance and poverty faster than ever in human history now offers the people of Europe easier escape. They require no physical movement or cultural risks experienced by their forebears.

Within Europe the free trade of the new Union offers escape from national governments that would limit freedoms of trade. The outlawing of hand-guns in Britain has been diminished by the ability of the citizen to escape by joining gun clubs in nearby France without moving home. More such escapes will limit the power of national governments to destroy the freedom of their citizens.

There is now increasing escape from British government services of all kinds, not least medical care, insurance of all kinds, even education and housing.

The latest domestic, home-bound 'New World' that science has opened out in the last two decades could raise world-wide living standards even faster. It has vastly accelerated the rate at which the simpler telephone and radio of the early and mid-20th century began to link Old Europe with New Europe without moving hearth and home.

The recently formed Union of Old Europe has virtually freed the citizens of the nation states of Europe from the danger of internal friction from political nationalism and economic protectionism that disfigured Europe after the First World War. The danger remains of protectionism against the outside world. Better than the European Union would be a North Atlantic Union of Old and New Europe in which all the nation states in both Continents renounced trade barriers between themselves.

If a North Atlantic Union is not formed the political powers of the nation states of Europe will be escaped by the resort to trading by electronic money, barter or the multiplying new devices that ease the rejection of oppressive national laws and invasive taxes.

Part IV:

From Political Democracy To Individual Liberty

19. Democracy at Bay

The cordial relationships between democratic government and the people as voters, customers and taxpayers have deteriorated.

The power of the people in democracy has grown in their three roles as citizens.

- As voters they are the ultimate rulers who no longer have to accept representatives who fail to interpret their interests.

- As consumers they can increasingly reject government that produces services they no longer want.

- And as taxpayers they can increasingly escape paying for services they reject.

Democracy as it was developing with individual, family and spontaneous group initiatives has been misled by political democracy into over-expanding the small sector of necessarily collective association. The people can now increasingly escape from them, but government cannot withdraw them because of the obstruction of its beneficiaries.

The political process of democracy has impaired the power of the people to learn from experience in protecting themselves from both irregular, unquantifiable uncertainty and recurring insurable risk. This is the historic failure of democracy: it has prevented or discouraged the people from learning from the discovery process of the market. It has confused the few services that for a time may have required to be collectivised in the state from the many which could better have been personalised through the market.

Democratic over-government is now belatedly rediscovering the mechanisms of personalised insurance that the people were discovering and developing but the state irresponsibly discouraged and almost suppressed until growing incomes, technology and tax rejection compelled it lately to confess failure and abjectly appeal to the people to resume the self-propelled private insurance proliferating in the market.

20. The New Mercantilism

Democracy is searching for new solutions to avoid over-government. The latest is a variant of the medieval mercantilism in Europe from the early 16th to the end of the 18th century.

The medieval notion of the supposed advantages of exporting more than importing in order to produce inflows of gold money developed political coalitions in the 16th-17th century Parliaments that are echoed in the present-day advantages, claimed by politicians and academics, for linking state and economic life in a 'third way'.

Medieval government that paternalistically regulated the detail of industry seemed to work more or less harmoniously with the early merchant venturers. The 'system', analysed by the Swedish economist Eli Heckscher in his masterly 1931 study, *Mercantilism*, was soon abandoned when, as with all national 'planning', it became too centralised and rigid to suit the rapid pace of the Industrial Revolution in the new vigorous markets of the late 18th century.

The classical economists especially revealed mercantilism as inadequate to facilitate faster economic advance. Adam Smith's *The Wealth of Nations* in 1776 was essentially a powerful intellectual and philosophic broadside against mercantilism. And it eventually gave way to the inadequate and short-lived yet powerful 40 years of freer trading in the mid-19th century.

Recent developments have seen a new liaison between historically hostile state government and private industry. The great debate of our times has been on the relationship between government and market, between political power and economic law, the power of government resting on law and the power of the people to better their condition in competitive markets.

The 1997 Government echoes the mercantilist anxiety to advise, admonish or regulate the details of industry for 'the public good'. Four conflicts of interest emerge.

First, government power over the conduct of industry can restrain the instinct of entrepreneurial minds to react promptly to market opportunities at home and overseas. The political mind cannot absorb the flexible reactions suited to the economic potential of the future. The predictable regularity in the 'chaos' of free scientific invention can be discovered only by the market.

Second, imposed conditions of employment in hours or rates of pay in industry, or other politically convenient acts of mercantilism, conflict with the interest of the owning shareholders who provide the savings for capital investment. Small shareholders, now often from working-class backgrounds, will look to the expertise of the institutional investors to protect them from political promises that cannot be honoured.

Third, government that increasingly hopes for private monies to rescue its failing projects, not least state education, must expect to pay exceptional yields for the exceptional risks of enterprises run by 'public officials' with no experience of the skills acquired in competitive markets.

And, *fourth*, the false trail of vaguely defined external 'stakeholders' conflicts with the interest of the owners – from wealthy shareholders to small investors in unit trusts, life assurance or lately ordinary shares in 'mutual' organisations – who risk the loss of their savings.

All these interests are reconciled in the market, which outlasts its politicised alternatives because no-one can easily escape the services of the state but all can stay with or exit from the market at will. As a political coalition the market is inherently unstable. If it were kept together by the coercive power of the state it would intensify the instinct of all parties – investors, shareholders, managers, workers, consumers – to escape from its regulations and taxes.

All 'stakeholders' would see themselves as rivals for the goodwill of the state. Such a contest for political favouritism was feasible in the slow-moving mercantilist middle ages. They would soon succumb to the age of ambitious scientific, industrial or financial innovators.

21. Too Late to Withdraw

The central question is whether democracy has indulged political importunity too long to be able to resist the barnacles and other obstacles to its withdrawal from over-government.

Winston Churchill retorted to the post-war mood of 'freeing the colonies': 'I am not here to preside over the dissolution of the British Empire.'

Government will now find not only that it must relax its economic empire. It must, more humbly, accept that it has lost the power to maintain it. The escapable power of political government meets the irresistible economic force of the market.

The remaining decision is to arrange its retreat with dignity before the escapes multiply to deprive it of the authority to influence the rate of its withdrawal.

The power remaining to government turns on the ability of politicians to recognise their weakening influence. Before long there will be increasing public understanding that the expansion in the state over the decades was unnecessary. The possibility must remain that the ability of government to command the economy can be by-passed not only by crudely breaking its laws and refusing its taxes, which recent evidence indicates may grow. The more constructive reaction would be to open markets everywhere: that is the only way to produce, much faster than political machinery, the new goods and services expected by the increasing numbers of rising incomes.

Government production may have coped with annual pre-war rises in real income in some years of 1.5 per cent doubling every 40 years or the post-war 2.5 per cent doubling in 25 years. It will be no match for future annual 4.5 per cent rises doubling every 15 years.

The people have rarely been able to determine what government 'should' do by awarding or withholding their votes. They can now more fundamentally decide what government can do by supplying or denying taxes and taking spending decisions outside its powers.

22. The Solution

Democracy has finally confessed it has lost the power – and moral authority – to finance (pay for) its inferior, dispensable, low quality, outdated services. Its politicised 'public' goods, its politicised public 'utilities', its politicised 'social' services, its politicised local authority services: all have to be subjected to the test of the market if they are to continue.

Government validated by the test of the market in the 21st century would satisfy the 17th-century Thomas Hobbes who left the long-taught warning that the excesses of the over-zealous sovereign were likely to be less malign than the mayhem of society without government. The 20th century knew the excesses of over-zealous government in the brutal dictatorships as well as in the benign welfare states.

Economists have long sought to discover the forces that determine the size of government. Several have left legacies of the solution that seemed important in their times.

The German Adolf Wagner in the late 19th century saw government as intent to increase its weight as national resources expanded. The British Professor Alan Peacock and his collaborator, the late Jack Wiseman, in 1961 traced over several decades the increases in government authority during wars but the reluctance to withdraw when peace could dispense with its increased powers. The American William Baumol in 1967 saw government as intent upon enlarging its proportion of the national product in order to maintain its 'public services' because its productivity tended to fall behind that of the private sector. And the American Professor Gordon Tullock in 1967 emphasised the growing power of pressure groups – 'rent-seekers' – to extract increased expenditure from democratic government.

These, and some other, theories explained some or much of the growth of government in the periods when they were evolved. The emphasis here is on the recent increases in the influences – including rent-seeking – making for over-government and the even more recent increases, or hitherto under-emphasised expansion, in the 'escapes' from over-government.

It is their recent confrontation – between escapable power and irresistible force – that has brought the new inability of government to maintain its supremacy over the market and provoked the dilemma of democracy.

The warnings of philosophers have not always been wise. Thomas Hobbes's warning was inadequate. His *Leviathan* declared that without sovereign authority there could be no state. 21st century democracy will have to rule with modest authority that reflects the general will. Without such reticence no legal authority will ensure popular observance. To echo Benedict de Spinoza: the sovereign has moral authority to exercise legal power so respectful of its subjects that they regard rebellion as worse than obedience.

COMMENT

by Sir Samuel Brittan

Arthur Seldon's essay on over-government is a characteristically thoughtful piece of work. It reveals a deep belief in the superior ability of ordinary citizens to make their own choices and decisions better than governments or experts or committees of the great and the good can make for them on their behalf.

Seldon's emphasis on the poor quality and lack of citizen choice in government services, interestingly enough, finds an echo among critics on the Left (and among Liberals with a capital 'L') who complain that these services are 'underfunded'. The difference lies in the remedies suggested. Left Wing critics bemoan the cowardice of governments in refusing to raise taxes to meet public demand for higher quality health and education – not to speak of the arts and myriads of other good causes. Seldon hopes for improvement by reducing taxes and leaving citizens to make their own arrangements.

What does the public want? It is difficult to dismiss out of hand multitudes of opinion surveys in which a large majority say they prefer improved services to lower taxes. It is human nature for people to want more of the services which they think that they, or their family or associates, are likely to need and to envisage tax increases which mainly fall on others. It is also natural to exaggerate the amount of improvement comparatively small tax increases – such as the 1p on the basic rate of tax advocated by the Liberal Democrats – might provide.

Governments of both main parties have tried to adopt a middle way. Conservatives promise – not always very convincingly – to edge the public spending ratio (measured by General Government Expenditure) below 40 per cent by scrutiny of detail, without touching the basic fabric of the Welfare State. Labour promises to improve public services without going above the magic 40 per cent level by transferring funds from social security to health and education. Again it is not quite clear how – except by taking advantage of a transitory upward phase in the business cycle. Neither side – not even when Margaret Thatcher was prime minister – has had the stomach for radical experiments.

Is there not a way past this impasse? A limited reform is possible by means of the purchaser-provider split eloquently championed by Evan Davis.[1] The principle is to maintain public finance for education and health but to encourage competition among suppliers, who could be in the private sector. There is still a lot going for this idea despite the bureaucrats' paradise produced by the last government in the Health Service. Nevertheless, even if well implemented, expenditure would still be determined by what governments think they can raise in taxes rather than by what citizens are prepared to pay directly.

A more radical route has been developed by John Willman in the case of the Health Service.[2] This is to maintain a basic core of state provision, but to raise more funds by charges and by encouraging users to purchase extra services, for instance amenity hospital beds, by direct payments. These two approaches could be complementary.

The innovative feature of Seldon's work is that he does not just bemoan the size of the tax and public spending burden, but lists the increasing number of ways which people are finding of escaping from it into the 'parallel economy'. This has already led governments all over the world to limit their ambitions in this area. Even pro-public sector political parties now emphasise the moderation of their ambitions and claim instead that they can squeeze more resources for popular services by careful choice of priorities. Very few governments, however, are prepared to embrace anything resembling the 20 per cent public spending ratio advocated by Seldon.

Nevertheless, his underlying analysis strikes a chord with many people of the most diverse views. The Internet itself is simply a means of communication, like the telegraph and the telephone. But in conjunction with capital mobility and the increased labour mobility promised by the European Single Market, it is taking us on a march towards a genuinely

---

[1] Evan Davis, *Public Spending*, London: Penguin, 1998.

[2] John Willman, *A Better State of Health*, London: Profile, 1998.

international economy – a march which was brought to a halt by the First World War, but which is now being resumed.

The same vista was seen by the Austrian Chancellor, Viktor Klima, when he took over the EU Presidency in July 1998, but he expressed it as an apprehension. He feared a competitive race to the bottom in European tax rates unless the EU took vigorous steps to harmonise. Charles Leadbeater writes in *The New Statesman*: 'Tax havens, once the preserve of the rich, will soon be in reach of anyone armed with a PC and a modem.'[3]

Should we celebrate this erosion of the taxing power or should we view it with alarm? If we were confident that the result would be the elimination of prestige projects ranging from the Concorde in the 1960s to the Dome or the unnecessary 'fast' Eurotunnel link through London today, and this were combined with a bold attempt to seek supplementary private sources of finance for valued services such as education and health, we could afford to cheer.

But there is another function of the state which at least some economic liberals find legitimate. This is to re-channel income and wealth towards the less well off. There is nothing sacrosanct about the distribution of wealth and income produced by the combination of the luck of inheritance and the market. Indeed, nobody was more insistent that these did not and could not represent a just pattern than that great champion of free markets, F. A. Hayek.

The way to introduce correctives is certainly not by interfering with market rewards by counter-productive devices such as the minimum wage. It is to devise a framework of rules, including if necessary redistributive taxation and transfers. The aim should not be to produce equality or to pursue the chimera of 'fair reward'. It should simply be to redistribute some counters towards those who have had bad luck in the market game. This is not the place to discuss how far we should go in this direction. I simply put in a marker here as I discuss the matter in more detail in a forthcoming study for the David Hume Institute.[4] A previous book of mine had a chapter entitled 'Redistribution – Yes, Equality – No'.[5]

---

[3] Charles Leadbeater, 'Goodbye, Inland Revenue', *New Statesman*, 3 July 1998.

[4] Samuel Brittan, *Essays: Moral, Political and Economic*, to be published for the David Hume Institute by Edinburgh University Press, 1998.

[5] Samuel Brittan, *Capitalism with a Human Face*, London: Fontana, 1996.

I doubt if a moderate amount of taxation for this purpose and to finance a core of basic education and health would itself lead to mass migration from countries imposing it. What is all too likely, however, is a cost ineffective mixture of public spending driven by traditional reflexes and interest group pressures, which will be high enough to impede economic performance but will not adequately deal with poverty.

The old textbook distinction between public spending on goods and services and transfer payments needs to be reinstated. In contrast to most politicians, and indeed some IEA authors, my own view is that there is a much stronger case for transfer payments than for direct expenditure on state services.

Clearly there is a great deal of 'churning' in the present tax and transfer system. In other words, many households pay out in taxes and contributions on the one hand and receive offsetting cash benefits on the other. But although a negative income tax could bring about a big simplification, let us not exaggerate the impact of a purely administrative change. What matters is the net payment to, or from, the citizen to the state.

At this point I must caution against an excessive emphasis on the public spending ratio as a measure of state intrusion on the individual. This is far from just being a technical measurement matter. Let us suppose that some government screwed up its courage and introduced educational vouchers in a big way, so that parents could exercise more choice. (And I would hope that older pupils would also have some say in their use. Children are individuals and not just possessions of their parents.)

Taxes would still have to be raised to finance the vouchers; and the public spending ratio would not necessarily fall. Or take Frank Field's idea of transferring more of the burden of providing for pensions to individual insurance. If provision is voluntary there has indeed been a transfer from collective to individual decision. But, if as Field apparently envisages, such provision is compulsory, then it continues to have much of the quality of taxation, irrespective of the exact funding mechanism.

Or take another example. Let us suppose that the Working Families Tax Credit (WFTC) is eventually developed into a negative income tax. Whether public spending is reduced or increased will depend on whether the payment is counted as positive public spending or negative taxation. The Treasury and the Office of National Statistics are, at the time of writing, locked in conflict on this very issue. Yet an accounting decision of this kind is hardly a basis for judging a bold move to substitute in-work benefits for the dole.

Or take a very different area: the Private Finance Initiative, under which private enterprise contracts to build schools, hospitals, battleships or whatever. The initial capital expenditure does not count as public spending at all, even under the widest definition. But the true cost will eventually come home to roost when governments have to make payments to companies for the use of these structures. As Davis has suggested, there should be a prominent note in the public expenditure documents of accumulated liabilities of this kind and their estimated implications for future current expenditure. Otherwise we may be building a trap for taxpayers not many years hence.

It is incidentally worth stressing how harmful the political emphasis on the basic rate of income tax has been to the cause of smaller government. There may be many arguments for the switch from direct to indirect taxes; but it is also an ideal way of disguising the true tax burden by hiding it in the price of goods in the shops. A 23p basic rate of tax does not seem all that much. But add in National Insurance Contributions (both employer and employee), excise taxes, VAT, council tax and other imposts; and the true marginal rate is more like 50 or 60 per cent.

In the end, what really matters is the proportion of their income that citizens are able to spend at their own discretion and how much is spent for them collectively. If the latter proportion is too high, then they are just left like children with pocket money. But the public spending ratio is too crude to be even an approximation to this percentage.

July 1998 SAMUEL BRITTAN
Financial Times

REFERENCES

Barro, Robert J., *Getting it Right, Markets and Choices in a Free Society*, The Massachusetts Institute of Technology Press, 1996.

Beenstock, Michael, 'Unemployment Insurance without the State', in *Reprivatising Welfare: After the Lost Century*, IEA Readings No. 45, London: The Institute of Economic Affairs, 1996, pp. 51-61.

Bohm-Bawerk, Eugen von, *Macht oder Okonomisches Gesetz*, 1914, *Shorter Classics of B.-B.*, Libertarian Press, USA, 1962.

Brittan, Sir Samuel, *Towards a Humane Individualism*, John Stuart Mill Institute, 1998.

Coase, R.H., *Essays on Economics and Economists*, Chicago & London: University of Chicago Press, 1994.

Dahl, Robert A., 'Democracy', in Bogdanor, V. (ed.), *Encyclopaedia of Political Institutions*, Oxford: Blackwell, 1987.

Daley, Janet, 'The Real Beneficiaries of Government Spending through the Arts Council', *The Daily Telegraph*, 17 March 1998.

de Jasay, Anthony, *Against Politics*, London: Routledge, 1997.

Eatwell, Lord, Milgate, M., Newman, P. (eds.), *The New Palgrave Dictionary of Economics*, London: Macmillan, 1987.

Ebenstein, Alan, *The Collected Works of Edwin Cannan*, Routledge-Thoemmes, 1997.

European Commission, *Communication on Undeclared Work*, reported in *The European*, 6-12 April 1998.

Fernandez-Armesto, F., *Millenium, A History of our Last 1000 Years*, New York: Bantam Press, 1995.

Fleming, Stewart, 'The Friendly Shall Inherit the Poor', *New Statesman*, 19 September 1997.

Furedi, Frank, 'Obsessed by Safety', *Daily Mail*, 13 December 1997.

Garelli, Stephane (ed.), *The World Competitiveness Report*, Lausanne, Switzerland, 1995.

Gates, Bill, 'The Web Lifestyle', in Fishburn, D. (ed.), *The World in 1998*, The Economist Publications, 1997.

Giddens, Anthony, 'The Third Way', *New Statesman*, 1 May 1998.

Green, David, 'Medical Care without the State', in *Reprivatising Welfare: After the Lost Century*, IEA Readings No. 45, London: The Institute of Economic Affairs, 1996, pp. 21-37.

Greenspan, Alan, 'Regulating Electronic Money', Cato Policy Report, March/April 1997.

Hayek, F.H., *The Denationalisation of Money*, IEA Hobart Paper 'Special' No. 70, London: The Institute of Economic Affairs, 1976, 2nd Enlarged Edition 1978.

Hobbes, Thomas, *Leviathan*, 1651, Everyman's Library, 1914.

Kirzner, I.M., *How Markets Work: Disequilibrium, Entrepreneurship and Discovery*, IEA Hobart Paper No. 133, 1997.

Landes, D.S., *The Wealth and Poverty of Nations*, Little Brown, 1998.

Parker, P., and Stacey, R., *Chaos, Management and Economics*, IEA Hobart Paper No. 125, 1994.

Peacock, A.T. and Wiseman, J., *The Growth of Public Expenditure in the United Kingdom, 1890-1955*, New Haven, Conn.: Princeton University Press, 1961.

Peacock, Sir Alan, *The Political Economy of Economic Freedom*, Edward Elgar, 1997.

Robinson, C., *A Policy for Fuel?*, IEA Occasional Paper 31, 1969.

Robinson, C., *The Energy 'Crisis' and British Coal*, IEA Hobart Paper No. 59, 1974.

Robinson, C., and Marshall, E., *Can Coal be Saved?*, IEA Hobart Paper No. 105, 1985.

Rowan, Wingham, *Guaranteed Electronic Markets*, London: Demos, 1997.

Schneider, Friedrich, 'The Shadow Economies of Western Europe', *Economic Affairs*, Vol. 17, No. 3, IEA, September 1997.

Seldon, A. (with F. G. Pennance), *Everyman's Dictionary of Economics*, London: J.M.Dent, 1965, Expanded Edition, 1975.

Seldon, A. (ed.), *The Long Debate on Poverty*, IEA Readings No. 9, 1972.

Seldon, A., *Charge*, Temple Smith, 1976.

Seldon, A. (ed.), *Tax Avoision*, IEA Readings No. 22, 1979.

Seldon, A., *Wither the Welfare State*, IEA Occasional Paper No. 60, 1981.

Seldon, A., 'Hypothetical Markets in Non-Public Goods', Center for Research in Government Policy, University of Rochester, Interlaken, 1985.

Seldon, A., *Capitalism*, Blackwell, 1990.

Seldon, A., *The State is Rolling Back*, Economic and Literary Books & IEA, 1994.

Seldon, A., Foreword to Ebenstein, Alan (ed.), *The Collected Works of Edwin Cannan*, Routledge-Thoemmes, 1997.

Seldon, A., 'From the LSE to the IEA', *Economic Affairs*, Vol. 18, No. 1, IEA, March 1998.

Seldon, M., in Radnitzky, G. (ed.), *Values and the Social Order*, Vol. 3, Avebury, 1997.

Shenfield, A. A., *The Political Economy of Tax Avoidance*, IEA Occasional Paper No. 24, 1968.

Shugarth II, W.F. (ed.), Foreword by McCracken, P.W., *Taxing Choice*, The Independent Institute, California, 1997.

Spencer, Herbert, *The Man versus the State*, Liberty Fund edition, 1982.

Spinoza, Benedict de, quoted in Lindsay, A. D., Introduction to Thomas Hobbes, *Leviathan*, J. M. Dent, 1914.

Sullivan, Andrew, 'It's a Wonderful Web Life', *Sunday Times*, 15 March 1998.

NOTE ON TRENDS AND STATISTICS ON THE PARALLEL ECONOMY

Most academic writings on European or world development that offer judgment on general or quantitative trends quote 'official' government statistics but rarely 'unofficial' quantitative evidence on recent or current trends in economic life.

'Official' sources have three main weaknesses: they are congenitally unreliable, often misleading and mostly backward-looking.

- They are *unreliable* because, like all government statistics, they are prone to political influence. They do not always state their contents or omissions; and they may be published too late to facilitate questioning of government policy.

- They are usually *inaccurate* because they omit or under-state the growing 'unofficial' economy. They understate trends in private and therefore total national incomes (GNP), productivity, investment, imports and exports. And they therefore over-state short-term fluctuations in unemployment and long-term poverty and inequality.

- Official statistics that form the basis for policy-making are still mostly *backward-looking*. The most revealing evidence is that the post-war welfare state was based largely on pre-war researches into the social conditions of the 1920s and 1930s. Some recent reforms of the 1997 Government are based on the supposed successes or relevance of post-war welfare reforms.

Government statistics cannot therefore be sufficient basis for judgment on economic performance, trends or prospects.

Judgements can be reinforced by three private sources of information and statistics on 'unofficial' developments and trends in economic life.

- Trends are studied in Reports with statistical estimates from European and North American research institutes.

- Latest developments in some detail are reported in the British and other press.

- The fullest estimates of elements or indications of developments in the 'unofficial' parallel economy are assembled in recent or coming Reports by academic economists and researchers. For example:

(i) Garelli, Stephane, *The World Competitiveness Report*, I.M.D., Lausanne, and World Economic Forum, Geneva, 1995.

(ii) Johnson, B.T. & Sheehy, T.P., *1996 Index of Economic Freedom*, Heritage Foundation, Washington DC, 1996.

(iii) Gwartney, J. D., and Lawson, R. A., *Economic Freedom of the World 1997*, Fraser Institute, Vancouver, with 47 co-publishers world-wide in Europe and other continents (avaliable from the IEA).

(iv) Schneider, F., 'The Shadow Economies of Western Europe', *Economic Affairs*, Vol. 17, No. 3, September 1997, London: The Institute of Economic Affairs, and other papers referenced therein.

The latest developments are increasingly reported in the British and world press, with informative details and graphic titles; recent examples in date order:

The Daily Telegraph, 'The Government's Taxing Dilemma', 19 September 1997.

Daily Mail, 'Bartering Bonanza, 40,000 escape taxman by working for each other', 15 November 1997.

Economist, The World in 1998, 'The World's Black Economy', 1998.

The Times, 'Questions of Tax and Moral High Ground', 26 March 1998.

The Times, 'Russia Plays the Generation [Cash] Game', 2 April 1998.

The European, commentaries on European Commission report, *Communication on Undeclared Work*, 12-18 April 1998.

Does The Past Have a Future?
The Political Economy of Heritage

Many countries are proud of their 'heritage,' in terms of buildings and various artefacts from the past. In some cases, a country's heritage is of such interest that people will travel long distances to view it.

But there are resource costs in preserving the past and presenting it: the resources so employed could have been used in other activities. How are decisions made about what should be preserved and how should those decisions be made?

In Does the Past have a Future?, eight distinguished authors (from France, Italy, Switzerland, the United Kingdom and the United States) examine such questions and consider alternative means of making preservation decisions, ranging from voting rights for citizens to various forms of privatisation.

The collection of papers is edited by Sir Alan Peacock, who is internationally known for his work on these issues.

1. The Economist and Heritage Policy: A Review of the Issues
   Sir Alan Peacock
2. Public Choice, Cost Benefit Analysis and The Evaluation of Cultural Heritage
   Bruno Frey and Felix Oberholzer-Gee
3. Heritage Regulation: A Political Economy Approach
   Ilde Rizzo
4. The Evolution of Heritage Policies: The Case of France
   Françoise Benhamou
5. The National Trust: The Private Provision of Heritage Services
   David Sawers
6. Museums and Galleries: Storehouses of Value
   Sir Gerald Elliot
7. International Aspects of Heritage Policies
   Dick Netzer

The Institute of Economic Affairs
2 Lord North Street, Westminster, London SW1P 3LB
Telephone: 0171 799 3745 Facsimile: 0171 799 2137
E-mail: iea@iea.org.uk Internet: http://www.iea.org.uk

£15.00

ISBN 0-255 36414-8

Regulating Financial Markets:

A Critique and some Proposals

George J. Benston

1. Financial services, financial firms and financial markets are regulated to a greater extent than most other products and services. Financial service regulation goes back centuries.
2. It provides benefits to governments (for example, from direct and indirect taxation of banks) and to regulated financial institutions (which gain where entry is restricted).
3. Consumer protection is a common reason given for financial regulation. But consumers in financial markets are probably less subject to fraud, misrepresentation, discrimination and information asymmetry than consumers of other products.
4. Concern about 'negative externalities' (costs borne by others) is another argument for regulation. However, on examination it is clear there are few genuine externalities.
5. Regulation on externality grounds is justified only for financial institutions which hold government-insured deposits; for insurance companies which provide government-mandated non-contracting third party insurance (for instance, for cars); and for companies which underwrite long-term life insurance and annuities.
6. Financial regulation incurs costs, borne by consumers and taxpayers, which probably exceed the benefits they receive. There are substantial unintended costs (such as reduced diversification of financial institutions and the absence of less costly and more innovative products because of restrictions on entry to financial markets).
7. An 'optimal regulatory system' for banks would involve substantial capital requirements, periodic reporting of assets, liabilities and capital and a 'structured early intervention' system for the authorities.
8. For government-mandated third party liability insurance, life insurance and annuities, insurance companies should be subject to capital requirements similar to those for banks.
9. If governments wish to protect consumers of financial products the best procedure is to establish an Ombudsman to which consumers who feel they have been mistreated can go.
10. The proposed regulatory system '...would be almost costless to taxpayers, the regulated companies and consumers of their products and services.' Compared with existing regimes, it has the great advantage of not restricting entry to financial markets nor the introduction of new products.

The Institute of Economic Affairs
2 Lord North Street, Westminster, London SW1P 3LB
Telephone: 0171 799 3745 Facsimile: 0171 799 2137
E-mail: iea@iea.org.uk Internet: http://www.iea.org.uk

£12.00

ISBN 0-255 36415-6